CH

GALILEO GALILEI

AND THE SCIENCE OF MOTION

GALILEO GALILEI
AND THE SCIENCE OF MOTION

William J. Boerst

MORGAN REYNOLDS
Publishing, Inc.

620 South Elm Street, Suite 223
Greensboro, North Carolina 27406
http://www.morganreynolds.com

RENAISSANCE SCIENTISTS

Nicholas Copernicus

Tycho Brahe

Johannes Kepler

Galileo Galilei

Isaac Newton

GALILEO GALILEI AND THE SCIENCE OF MOTION

Copyright © 2004 by William J. Boerst

Library of Congress Cataloging-in-Publication Data

Boerst, William J.
    Galileo Galilei and the science of motion / William J. Boerst.— 1st
ed.
        p. cm. — (Renaissance scientists)
Summary: Presents the life and work of the famous sixteenth-century
Italian astronomer and physicist.
Includes bibliographical references and index.
    ISBN 1-931798-00-1 (lib. bdg.)
    1. Galilei, Galileo, 1564-1642—Juvenile literature. 2.
Astronomers—Italy—Biography—Juvenile literature. 3.
Physicists—Italy—Biography—Juvenile literature. [1. Galilei, Galileo,
1564-1642. 2. Scientists.] I. Title. II. Series.
    QB36.G2B62 2004
    520'.92—dc22

                        2003014191

With love and appreciation to Julie and Joe

Special thanks to Professor Owen Gingerich for providing information relevant to the manuscript.

CONTENTS

CHAPTER ONE
LEARNING TO QUESTION

According to one of Galileo Galilei's early biographers, he made his first scientific discovery in 1583 when he was a student at the University of Pisa. While attending mass in the city cathedral, he became preoccupied with a heavy lamp on a chain swaying like a pendulum above the altar. As he watched it swing, he was surprised to notice that, although the length of the lamp's arc shortened at a consistent rate, the period, or amount of time it took the lamp to traverse the ever-smaller arcs, seemed to remain the same. This appeared contrary to common sense, which would suggest the arc's period would decrease along with its distance.

According to the story, Galileo placed a finger on his wrist and used his pulse to time the arcs. By applying this crude form of measurement, he was able to confirm

Opposite: Galileo Galilei by Ottavio Leoni. *(Courtesy of Musée du Louvre.)*

While observing the swinging of a chandelier similar to this one in the Pisa Cathedral, Galieo discovered the law of isochronism. *(Courtesy of the Pisa Cathedral.)*

that, regardless of the arc's length, its period remained constant, or—as a scientist would say—the arc's period was independent of its length. Later, scientists would realize this held true for short arcs only, but even so, it demonstrated to Galileo that preconceived ideas do not always stand up to objective analysis. Someone may have discovered the law of isochronism earlier, but this was a remarkable achievement for a young student.

No one knows for certain if this story is true, however, and this uncertainty indicates another important aspect of Galileo's life. He is one of history's most controversial figures, surrounded by both ardent supporters and equally ardent enemies. The story of his experiment in the cathedral first appeared in a biography written by a friend. It is possible the author invented, or exaggerated, the story to show Galileo in the best possible light.

Galileo is sometimes called the first modern scientist because he refused to accept any theory that had not been subjected to rigorous verification. He was the first modern scientist to consistently use experiments and measurement. He spent years asking questions about how physical forces operated on Earth—how did balls fall, why did ice float, what was the relationship between time and motion—and designed experiments to find answers. Although many of his discoveries in earth-bound physics ran counter to what had been taught for nearly two thousand years, these discoveries did not lead to his collision with the powerful Catholic Church. Not until he turned his attention to the heavens, becoming convinced by physical evidence that the Sun, not the Earth, was at the center of the universe, did he become so controversial that he was eventually tried as a heretic.

Galileo refused to stay in his laboratory and hide from controversy. He welcomed the opportunity to advocate his ideas and to publicize his findings, convinced that progress must be fought for. Although this attitude got him into trouble, it also insured that long after he was gone his work would remain part of the public discourse.

Galileo Galilei was born in Pisa, Italy, on February 15, 1564. The English playwright William Shakespeare was born the same year, and the artist Michelangelo died in Rome three days after Galileo's birth. Galileo was the eldest child in his family. Birth records survive for three of his siblings. His sister Virginia was born in 1573; a brother, Michelangelo, arrived in 1575; and the baby of the family, Livia, came into the world in 1587. There were four other children, although their names have been lost, indicating they died in infancy.

The Italy of Galileo's youth was not a unified nation but a collection of separate states with a variety of governments. Venice, for example, was a republic with an elected senate and a *doge*, or ruler for life, who was chosen by the senate. The Tuscany region, with its capital city of Florence, began as a republic with elected representatives. By the time of Galileo's birth, although it still maintained republican institutions, Tuscany was controlled by the powerful Medici family, who had risen to power with wealth accumulated in banking and trade.

The Renaissance—the French word for rebirth—is the name given to the revival of classical culture and the decline of medievalism that began in Italy during the fourteenth century. A combination of factors led to the development of the Renaissance in Italy. Most importantly, Italy was located at the center of the trade routes linking Western Europe to the East. This trade brought wealth and fostered the development of manufacturing, especially helping the textile business to flourish in Florence. The wealth was used to subsidize art and education. As well, the lack of a single, powerful government on the Italian peninsula also allowed for a freer development of the spirit of inquiry, in part because it was possible for an artist or intellectual who was out of

Galileo Galilei was born in this house in Pisa in 1564. His father, Vincenzio, worked as a musician and a teacher of music.
(Courtesy of Dr. G.B. Pineider, Florence, Italy.)

favor in one state to move to another. Galileo would move from Tuscany to Venice and back during his career, for example.

Finally, there were changes within the Catholic Church during the early modern era that influenced the Renaissance. These new thinkers, called humanists, began to reevaluate Catholic theology, emphasizing the potential of humans rather than their sinfulness, and celebrating life on Earth. To these new philosophers, humans were more than sinners, and life was more than a travail to be endured in hopes of one day reaching paradise in heaven.

These structural developments and new attitudes drew artists toward more secular subjects and themes. Raphael and Botticelli, for example, painted subjects from Greek mythology, and sculptors such as Michelangelo and Donatello mixed religious and secular themes in their art. Leonardo da Vinci, also a Florentine, was interested in practically everything he encountered. Da Vinci studied how birds fly and how to build better canal locks. He even figured out what makes walls crack. He dissected bodies and painted portraits and biblical scenes, including the *Mona Lisa* and *The Last Supper*.

Leonardo da Vinci was the classic "Renaissance man" who was both interested and accomplished in many different areas. In many ways, Galileo's father was also a "Renaissance man." Vincenzio Galilei made his money as a merchant most of his life, but his love was music. He worked as a musician and teacher, and wrote books on music theory that earned him a reputation as a radical who rejected any musical theory he did not think worked

Self-portrait of Leonardo da Vinci from 1512. *(Courtesy of Palazzo Reale, Turin, Italy.)*

in practice. He was also schooled in classical languages and mathematics. Vincenzio took a great interest in his oldest son and taught him to play the lute and to draw. The family lived in Pisa until 1572, when they relocated to Florence, where Vincenzio had an opportunity to adapt Greek tragedies to music.

Galileo stayed in Pisa with a wealthy uncle to continue his schooling after the family moved. He joined his parents in Florence in 1574. A precocious boy who had inherited his father's tendency to show off his intelligence, Galileo went to grammar school until the age of thirteen, when he attended a monastery for lessons in Greek, Latin, and logic. There, he expressed a desire to enter the Church. His father responded to this request by removing him from the monastery school and taking him back to Florence. Vincenzio had no intention of letting his brilliant son spend his life as a monk.

In September 1581, at age seventeen, Galileo returned to Pisa and, at his father's prompting, enrolled in the university as a medical student. Galileo's life, though, soon turned in a direction he would pursue until his death. In 1583, while home in Florence during a vacation, he met a family friend, Ostilio Ricci, who taught various technical courses at the Florentine art school. Ricci's first love was mathematics, and during the break from school, he introduced Galileo to the subject. Ricci not only taught the boy mathematics, he introduced him to the idea that quantification—measurement—should be used along with observation and logic as the preferred method of verifying scientific discoveries.

Galileo was intrigued and, after returning to school, began to neglect his medical classes to study mathematics. When his father learned of this, he traveled to Pisa to set his son back on the path of medicine. Galileo pleaded with Ricci to intervene with his father. Ricci, astounded at how quickly Galileo was learning the subject, believed the boy should be allowed to follow his dream, even though mathematics was not as highly

Ostilio Ricci persuaded Galileo's father to allow Galileo to continue his study of mathematics. *(Courtesy of Dr. G.B. Pineider, Florence, Italy.)*

respected as medicine, and any job teaching it would pay much less than a doctor earned.

Ricci took Vincenzio into a room for a private, lengthy conversation about the matter. When they finished talking, Vincenzio reluctantly agreed to let Galileo study mathematics at Pisa for one more year. After that, his son would be on his own unless he returned to medicine—something which Galileo had no intention of doing.

Ricci introduced Galileo to the works of Archimedes (287-212 B.C.), who was one of the first natural philosophers, or scientists, to quantify his experiments. Most famous for discovering the law of the lever and the law of buoyancy, he used mathematics to determine areas and to measure volumes in experiments. Archimedes soon became Galileo's guide for incorporating mathematics into science.

Galileo spent one more year at the University of Pisa before leaving in 1585. Because he had neglected his regular courses in medicine, he left without a degree. Back in Florence, his father's prediction that he would have a difficult time earning a living in his chosen field turned out to be true. He lived with his family for four years, trying to make a financial contribution by tutoring and other projects, but spent most of his time continuing his own education in mathematics, philosophy, and literature. He also assisted his father with experiments in musical harmony.

When Galileo began his own experiments, he followed Archimedes's example. At one point, he revisited Archimedes's most famous experiment, the discovery of the law of buoyancy. After studying how Archimedes had derived his law and confirming the methodology, he wrote his work up in a small pamphlet called *The Little*

Archimedes's theory of the lever began the science of mechanics. Legend has it that he boasted "Give me a place to stand and I will move the earth." *(Engraving from "Mechanics Magazine," London, 1824.)*

Balance. Although he only passed the pamphlet around among his friends, it impressed everyone who read it and helped him to build a reputation as a mathematician.

Galileo wrote other small treatises that were passed around among intellectuals. As he slowly became better known, he began to attract wealthy and influential supporters. He traveled to Rome with one such family in 1587, where he met several influential and wealthy men. In 1588, he was invited to give a series of lectures at the Academy of Florence about the topography of hell as described in the epic poem *The Divine Comedy,* by the medieval writer Dante. Galileo's lectures were well received.

Ironically, in light of the direction his life would eventually take, Galileo was passed over for a job teaching mathematics at the University of Bologna because he knew too little about astronomy. Astronomy was at that time a part of the mathematics curriculum. Disappointed at losing this prestigious job, Galileo called upon the influence of a powerful friend, Guidobaldo del Monte, whose brother was a cardinal. Del Monte arranged a position for Galileo at the University of Pisa. His job title was chairman of the mathematics department, the contract was only for three years, and the annual salary was a mere fraction of what a professor of medicine was paid. But it was a job in his chosen field. Galileo Galilei, now twenty-five, was returning to his old college, this time as a professor.

CHAPTER TWO
ON MOTION

Galileo had not been popular with his professors when he was a student at Pisa. He was not inclined to simply accept information that was presented to him without proof. He questioned his professors, and did so aggressively. This characteristic earned Galilieo the nickname of "the Wrangler."

Many of his old professors were still at the University of Pisa when Galileo returned as their colleague, and they were not happy to see him. When his arrival in Pisa was delayed because the Arno River flooded, which forced him to miss six lectures, the school administrators deducted a fine from his already meager salary. Before the year was out, he was again fined, this time

Galileo's first official teaching position was at the University of Pisa. He later claimed to have dropped balls from Pisa's famous Leaning Tower to determine whether objects of different weights fall at the same rate. *(Courtesy of the Library of Congress.)*

for refusing to wear the traditional scholar's gown. He thought the gown was impractical and, after paying the fine, wrote a three-hundred-line poem ridiculing the tradition. Among other complaints, the poem asserted that uniforms hid the true nature of an individual.

The tension between Galileo and his colleagues involved more than disagreements about dress, or Galileo's lack of tact. It was rooted in their approach to the study of the natural world, as well as the fundamental question of what scientific truth is and how it is best determined. These conflicting worldviews centered primarily on their differing attitudes toward the writings of the ancient Greek philosopher Aristotle.

Aristotle (384-322 B.C.) had attempted to organize the physical world into a coherent system. According to Aristotle, and the philosophers who revised his philosophy over the centuries, the universe was contained in a sphere, bordered on the outer edges by the stars, with Earth at the center. The closed, spherical universe was divided into two sections. The largest section, the celestial sphere, included the Moon and stretched to the outer edge of the enclosed universe. It was composed of only one element, aether. The smaller inner section, known as the sublunary sphere, included Earth and the area between our planet and the Moon. Aristotle believed nothing existed beyond the outer, stellar sphere.

The aether of the celestial sphere was believed to be transparent, pure, and changeless. Aristotle's followers thought the aether crystallized into fifty-five solid spheres in which the planets, Sun, stars, and Moon orbited the stationary Earth. These spheres were embedded in an interlocking system. The primary force for movement came from the outer sphere, which moved by its own volition and, through friction, caused the next sphere's circular orbit, which then moved the next sphere, and so on. Energy, then, was believed to originate on the periphery and moved inward.

Earth rested at the center of this system of crystalline spheres and at the core of the sublunary sphere. Instead of aether, there were four elements in the sublunary sphere—earth, air, water, and fire. The intermingling of these four elements was the fundamental difference between the celestial and sublunary spheres.

According to Aristotle, Earth was much more complicated and chaotic than the heavens, with each element trying to maintain its "natural" position relative to the others. Earth, for example, was the heaviest and inclined to settle at the center, while air, the lightest, attempted to settle into the outermost shell, and fire, the second lightest of the terrestrial elements, sought its home between air and water. For this reason, rocks tend to fall to earth, and flames rise up through air.

In Aristotle's system, the elements on Earth were constantly attempting to find their own unique resting place. If all the elements attained this goal simultaneously, he reasoned, all motion on Earth would cease, and the sublunary sphere would achieve a state of perfection like that found in the celestial sphere. In Aristotle's view, two kinds of motion existed. Both the circular motion of the heavens and the stillness of the elements at rest were known as "natural" motion. The mixing of the four earthly elements, however, allowed for unnatural, or "violent," motion. Violent motion resulted when an outside impetus propelled an object, as when an arrow is shot, a rock thrown, or a cannonball fired.

Because elements on Earth sought their natural resting places, linear motion would last only until the original impetus was exhausted. Once that happened, natural motion took over, and the object would immediately follow the dictates of its elemental composition, falling to the ground.

Aristotle's universe was a single, interlocking system in which heavier objects fell faster than lighter ones. He proposed that the rate of fall and the object's weight were

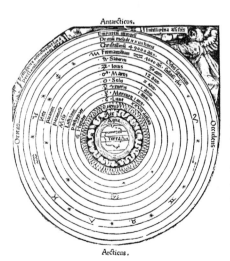

Aristotle developed a model of the universe made up of nested spheres, with the planets orbiting a central Earth. *(From Aristotle:* Libri de caelo. IIII. *Edited by Johann Eck, Augsburg, 1519.)*

directly proportional, so a ten-pound ball would fall twice as fast as a five-pound ball. The weight of an object was also indicative of its elemental composition.

Galileo had numerous questions and doubts about Aristotle's description of the universe. But it was the ancient philosopher's rejection of the use of mathematics in science that most offended him. Aristotle had rejected the arguments of Pythagoras and Plato, two thinkers who came before him who had said nature was written in numbers. Aristotle said numbers and geo-

PLATO

Plato was born in Athens around 427 B.C. He was devoted to his mentor, Socrates, and for several years after the death of his teacher, Plato wandered the settled areas of Greece, Northern Africa, and Italy studying Pythagorean theory. Pythagoras taught that the only way to truth was through numbers. When he returned to Athens, he established a school that came to be called the Academy, dedicated to the teaching of philosophy and mathematics. One of his students was Aristotle.

Plato's surviving writings consist of a series of dialogues. He subscribed to Pythagoras's theory that objects that can be seen and touched are not real. In this theory, only those things that cannot be seen or touched but can be apprehended with the mind are real, and it is only through abstract mathematics that this ideal can be understood.

Plato died in his sleep around 347. Following his death, the Academy continued until 529 A.D. Even after it closed, the philosophy of the Academy continued to be a strong influence, particularly in the development of Christian theology.

metrical shapes did not actually exist in nature but were constructs of the mind, that if the mind did not exist, neither would number and shape. He thought learning from mathematics was less valid and more dangerous than learning through our senses. It was less valid because it was not natural, and more dangerous because it merely gave the illusion of being conclusive.

As a young professor, Galileo's colleagues often ostracized him. This gave him ample time to begin a systematic analysis of what struck him as implausible about Aristotle's theories. He began by investigating the rate of falling bodies.

Galileo said he first began to question Aristotle's law of falling bodies when, as a boy, he watched large and small hailstones hit the ground at the same time. If Aristotle were right, shouldn't stones of different sizes be falling at different rates? Wouldn't the heavier stones hit the ground first? This was clearly not what happened. One possible solution was that some sort of synchronized system determined when the hailstones left the clouds, in effect timing when the stones fell so they all hit the ground at the same time. Or maybe the larger stones fell from more distant clouds.

More likely, Galileo reasoned, there was a simpler explanation—hailstones, regardless of weight, fall at the same rate. If this applied to hailstones, it would apply to all objects. But a feather, dropped from a high place, took longer to hit the ground than a rock. Galileo wondered if this was due to air resistance. If air resistance were eliminated, such as in a vacuum, would the two objects fall at the same speed? Rather than upholding the Aristotelian worldview, Galileo investigated one phenomenon at a time, allowing nature to speak for itself through mathematical analysis.

There is no way to know for sure if he ever performed the legendary experiment of dropping balls of different weights from the Leaning Tower of Pisa. We do know he used this idea as a "thought experiment" in his arguments. Aristotle said a ten-pound ball would fall ten times faster than a one-pound ball. Galileo asked his colleagues: "Try, if you can, to picture in your mind the large ball striking the ground while the small one is less than a yard from the top of the tower." What if, he asked, you joined two equal balls together and dropped them? Would that double the speed of their fall?

The story of the Leaning Tower demonstration came from an anecdote Galileo told a young friend late in his life. As he remembered it years later, the heavier ball beat the smaller ball by a mere two inches. Galileo knew this was because of air resistance, but his many enemies claimed it as proof that Aristotle was right. Galileo was incredulous:

> Aristotle says that a hundred-pound ball falling from a height of a hundred *braccia* (arm lengths) hits the ground before a one-pound ball has fallen one *braccio*. I say they arrive at the same time. You find, on making the test, that the larger ball beats the smaller one by two inches. Now, behind those two inches you want to

hide Aristotle's ninety-nine *braccia* and, speaking only of my tiny error, remain silent about his enormous mistake.

Undercutting Galileo's attempt to prove Aristotle wrong during his years at the University of Pisa was a mistake that he would later fix. At this early stage, he thought there was a limit to which a falling body could accelerate. He would later discover that the speed continues to increase. At this point, however, he was still enough of an Aristotelian to think that the earthly elements in a body worked as a counterforce to gravity. In other parts of his unpublished essay, *On Motion*, he wrote on the subject, recording some of the experiments he had conducted by rolling balls down an inclined

Ptolemy refined Aristotle's system to more accurately match the movements of the planets, Moon, and Sun. *(From Hevelius: Selenographia, 1647.)*

plane. (It was easier to measure the speed of fall when a ball was rolled down an inclined plane than when it was dropped.) His goal was to find the ratio of time and distance for a falling body. Galileo also questioned Aristotle's division of motion into natural and unnatural. These questions would remain central to his work for decades.

Although *On Motion* was never published, and the manuscript was read by only a few people, it demonstrates Galileo's early commitment to the scientific method, including the use of mathematics, as the best way to quantify experimental results and arrive at hypotheses. It was the refusal of the Aristotelians to experiment, or to accept the results of his experiments, that he found so frustrating. To many of the Aristotelians, Galileo was a stuntman. They did not care what he deduced from his rolling balls and mathematical scribbling. They were not going to throw away two thousand years of revered wisdom to put their trust in a man who even ridiculed the wearing of the scholar's robe.

Galileo spent a great deal of his time as a professor at Pisa developing a procedure for doing "thought experiments." He would think through an experiment as though it were being done in a perfect environment, such as testing falling bodies in a vacuum, then he would apply mathematical analysis to quantify what he thought would happen. Later, he would use this method to develop hypotheses to be tested by physical experiments.

At Pisa, Galileo primarily occupied himself with work

Guidobaldo del Monte, an influential member of the Tuscan nobility, helped Galileo secure his first teaching position at the University of Pisa. *(Courtesy of Dr. G.B. Pineider, Florence, Italy.)*

in the mechanics of force and motion on Earth, as had his hero Archimedes. When he taught astronomy, as his duties required, he stuck with the principles of Ptolemy, who had established a cosmological system based upon the Aristotelian two-sphere system, with Earth in the center, because it was the heaviest, and the Sun and other planets rotating around Earth in circular orbits. If Galileo had begun to wonder about the viability of Aristotle's physics in the heavens, as he did on Earth, he kept his doubts to himself for the time being.

In 1591, Galileo's seventy-year-old father died. Now, as the oldest son, Galilieo was financially responsible for his mother, for the dowry payments that were necessary to find his sisters husbands, as well as for the care of his sixteen-year-old brother, Michelangelo. He could not meet all these responsibilities on his salary, which was barely enough to support one person.

When Galileo told Guidobaldo del Monte, who had

helped him get the position in Pisa, about his financial pressures, Guidobaldo arranged for him to receive the chair of mathematics at the University of Padua. The job came with a four-year contract, and a renewal clause for another two years. The starting salary was still not sufficient for his needs, but he could expect regular raises. Most importantly, Padua was located in the Venetian Republic, where there was a more open spirit of inquiry. It would be a more hospitable place for "the Wrangler" to work and teach.

Galileo gave his first lecture in Padua in December 1592. He was twenty-eight. Determined to make a good impression, he worked hard on the lecture, and it was a success. Although most of his classes were in geometry, he also taught astronomy. Medical students were required to study astronomy, as physicians of the period used the stars and planets to help diagnose illnesses. Galileo used Johannes Sacrobosco's *Sphere,* which relied on Ptolemy's Earth-centered model, as the astronomy textbook.

CHAPTER THREE
STARRY MESSENGER

Galileo later described his years in Padua (1592-1610) as the happiest of his life. He had friends and supportive colleagues on the staff. One of his closest friends during this time was Cesare Cremonini who, ironically, was a defender of Aristotle. (Followers of Aristotle were often called Peripatetics—"one who walks around"—which referred to Aristotle's reputed habit of walking while he lectured.) Although Galileo and Cremonini disagreed about physics, they had a deep mutual respect and enjoyed one another's company.

Another friend, Benedetto Castelli, was his student in Padua. He went on to become an advisor to the pope and would play a prominent role in Galileo's later life, in-

The city of Padua was located in the Venetian Republic. The University of Padua, the largest university in Europe, was one of the intellectual centers of the Renaissance. *(From Hartmann Schedel:* World View, *1493.)*

cluding his conflict with the Church. Another colleague, Paolo Sarpi, wrote on many subjects, but concentrated on politics and theology. He advocated stricter limitations of the pope's power, which was a hot issue of the time. Many of the secular rulers bristled at the power the pope and the Church had to interfere in their affairs.

The University of Padua was the largest university in Europe, and it was noted for its tradition of academic freedom and free expression. Nicholas Copernicus, who had published a book in 1543 that argued the Sun, not Earth, was at the center of the universe, spent time there in the fifteenth century. William Harvey, the Englishman who discovered how the heart and circulatory system work, became a student in the medical school there a few years after Galileo began teaching.

Galileo's life nearly ended during his first summer in the city when he and friends escaped the heat by going into a cave located near a waterfall. Behind the waterfall was a conduit that allowed cool air to enter the cave. Although such cooling chambers were common, they were also dangerous because of the possibility of poisonous gas gathering in the unventilated areas. On this afternoon, the men fell asleep, and upon awakening, discovered they were suffering from cramps, chills, headaches, hearing loss, and a lack of energy. Two of the men died within days. Galileo survived, but was plagued with bouts of rheumatism, or arthritis, the rest of his life, possibly as a result of this experience.

Although his salary in Padua was higher than it had been in Pisa, it was still not adequate to meet his obligations. When his sister Virginia married in 1591, he had to provide the dowry—the fee paid to the groom's family—which took him several years to pay off. He promised a large dowry for his sister Livia to arrange for a suitable suitor, and his brother Michelangelo frequently needed money as he began a career as a musician.

Galileo was also beginning a family of his own. He had met Marina Gamba while visiting Venice, which was only thirty miles away. The two fell in love but were never married, an arrangement that was not uncommon for scholars, who often remained single due to their limited income. It is possible, too, that Galileo might have considered Marina, who came from a middle-class family, to be an unsuitable wife. Still, he assumed responsibility for her and the three children they eventually had together. He moved her from Venice to a house near his home in Padua. His daughter Virginia was born in 1600, Livia in 1601, and his son Vincenzio in 1606.

To help meet his expenses, Galileo moved into a large house near the university and rented rooms to students, a standard practice of professors at the time. He earned extra money by tutoring his boarders. Most of the students were destined to inherit large farms and needed help with practical skills in mathematics.

Financial pressure motivated Galileo to design, build, and sell scientific instruments. One of his biggest moneymakers involved the improvements he made to the proportional compass. The original instrument featured a pair of joined compasses that could be used to divide straight lines into sections. Galileo refined the instrument by adding more scales on the arms, which made it useful for working out squares and cubes, multiplying, and computing compound interest. Shipbuilders used it to test the strength of hulls and to measure the density of stones and other objects. To make the tool more versatile, he added a curved metal arc that joined the two right angles. This modification turned the instrument into a quadrant that could be used to measure heights and angles. Because it could be used to aim cannons, Galileo called it a military compass. He hired a local artisan named Marcantonio Mazolleni to work in his workshop, and over a ten-year period the two men made more than three hundred military compasses.

His instruments brought in money, but his biggest profits came from the fees customers paid to be taught how to use them. He wrote an instructional manual called *Operations of the Geometric and Military Compass of Galileo Galilei* that sold very well. He dedicated the manual to sixteen-year-old Cosimo de Medici, who was one of his private students. Cosimo was the heir to

Galileo considered Florence, the capital of the Republic of Tuscany, to be his hometown.

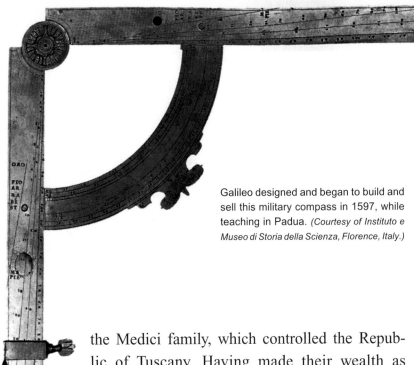

Galileo designed and began to build and sell this military compass in 1597, while teaching in Padua. *(Courtesy of Instituto e Museo di Storia della Scienza, Florence, Italy.)*

the Medici family, which controlled the Republic of Tuscany. Having made their wealth as merchants and bankers, the Medici was one of the most powerful families in Europe by the sixteenth century. They ruled over Florence almost like royalty. Galileo hoped the dedication to young Cosimo would help him someday receive an appointment as the Medici family mathematician, so that he could return home. His family had once been part of the Tuscan nobility, and the proud Galileo was determined to return to Florence someday.

The Venetian Republic, located in northeast Italy, was ruled with a much lighter hand than the Medici used in Florence. This more open attitude was due, in part, to the leaders of Venice, who had for years adopted an adversarial attitude towards the Church in Rome. During the years before Galileo came to Padua, the tensions between the republic and the Church almost led to war.

The Medici family, on the other hand, wanted to maintain their influence at the Vatican. Galileo took advantage of the more open atmosphere in Padua to record his ideas in manuscripts that he passed around among colleagues and students. He also gave public lectures that openly contradicted Aristotle.

Galileo began to publicly question Aristotle's distinction between "natural" motion, which Aristotle said was inherent in the elements, and the second kind of "violent" motion that occurred only on Earth. One question that Aristotle had not answered to Galileo's satisfaction was how a projectile kept moving forward once the initial impetus was gone. Why, for example, did an arrow continue to move after it left the bow? One suggestion was that the air the arrow displaced from its path gathered behind it and pushed it forward. But if the arrow was driven forward by displaced air, why did it not go on forever? Another popular suggestion was an arrow, once launched, was motivated by a new impetus created by the act of being in motion. When this secondary force burned out, the object fell to the ground. But why was this new acquired impetus so quick to burn out when the other elemental impulses did not?

Both theories were impossible to validate, and Galileo was convinced all natural laws could be mathematically verifiable. He was not concerned with developing another explanation out of thin air. He wanted to discover what actually happened.

Galileo would not solidify his thinking on the ques-

FALLING BODIES

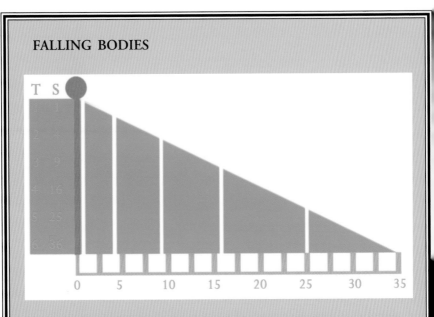

Galileo wanted an answer to the question: What is the rate of acceleration of a falling body? In his earlier work, he thought there was a limit to the rate of acceleration. By his last years, while working on *Two New Sciences*, he no longer held this belief.

Galileo performed his falling bodies experiments by building an inclined plane to roll the balls down. Because there was no standard measurement of time available, no accurate clocks, he also designed a water clock that released water at a controlled rate. He would then weigh the amount of water released to determine the duration period of the experiment. In effect, he weighed the time it took a ball to roll down an inclined plane. The watery results of several experiments were compared.

Using this method, Galileo determined that the distance the ball traveled from rest to stop was proportional to the squares of the time it took to traverse the distance, and acceleration remained uniform throughout the fall.

tion of motion until decades later, when he published *Two New Sciences* in 1638, near the end of his life. At this early stage, though, he had already rejected Aristotle's idea of two different types of motion. This was a critical first step toward the development of a single set of natural laws for the entire universe.

When he turned back to his work on falling bodies, Galileo determined the distance a ball traveled down an inclined plane was proportional to the square of the period after its release. He had discovered a proportional relationship between time and distance that held up regardless of the weight or composition of the object.

Galileo also renewed his work with pendulums. He measured the swing of a pendulum weighted at one end with balls of various sizes and weights. Doing this helped him confirm that the period of the swing was related not to the size and weight of the ball, but to the length of the pendulum. The time it took to complete a swing was proportional to the square of the pendulum's length. Again, time was proportional to distance. These discoveries contributed to the development of more accurate clocks.

Galileo did not limit his research to motion. He became intrigued by magnets and worked on ways to make them stronger. He experimented with measuring air temperature by warming a glass bulb with a long, thin neck and inverting it in water. The contraction of the warm air drew water into the neck, with the amount of drawn water dependent on the temperature of the bulb. This led to the development of a water thermometer.

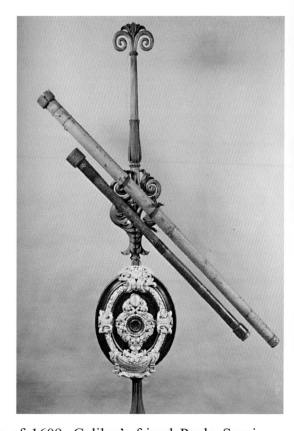

Galileo's design for a telescope greatly improved the instrument's efficiency. *(Courtesy of Instituto e Museo di Storia della Scienza, Florence, Italy.)*

In the summer of 1609, Galileo's friend Paolo Sarpi told him about a new instrument that was creating a sensation in the Netherlands. This new "seeing tube" magnified distant objects to nine times their actual size. Galileo realized the scientific and commercial possibilities of what would come to be called a telescope and began writing to friends all over Europe asking for information about it.

The first telescopes were of very poor quality. The lenses were poorly ground, and distant objects, while larger, were so blurry as to be almost indistinguishable.

Galileo convinced the Venetian Senate to buy his version of the telescope for use in military defense. *(Courtesy of The British Museum.)*

The poor quality threatened to reduce the telescope to the status of a novelty. When the doge, or ruler, of Venice considered purchasing one at an exorbitant price, both Sarpi and Galileo recommended against it.

Galileo knew the doge was considering purchasing the telescope to be used as a defensive tool by the military. Venice was a harbor city surrounded by water, and any attack would come from the sea. A telescope could be used to watch for approaching ships. Galileo set out to manufacture a better instrument than those he had seen. He ground new lenses from fine Venetian glass and adjusted the curvature of the two lenses, which increased their ability to magnify.

On August 21, 1609, he demonstrated his telescope for the doge and the Venetian senate. They gathered in the bell tower of St. Mark's Cathedral and took turns staring at the town of Padua, twenty-four miles away.

The senators were very impressed. One wrote of the "marvelous and effective singularity of the spy glass.

Anyone of us were able to see distinctly the campanile and cupola with the façade of the church of Saint Guistina in Padua."

The grateful Venetian Senate rewarded Galileo with a lifetime appointment as state mathematician and a generous salary of one thousand florins a year. He improved the design of the telescope and began manufacturing it for sale. His first large contract came from the Venetian government.

Galileo's discovery and use of the telescope is one of the most important events in his career. Before 1609, he spent little time on astronomy and still taught the Ptolemaic system to his students. He had, however, already engaged in a debate with an Aristotelian friend who had insisted much more of the sky would be visible if Earth were in motion. Using mathematics, Galileo demonstrated to his own satisfaction that his friend's argument lacked proof. Galileo's experiments in motion and other aspects of mechanics had convinced him that Aristotle's physics did not hold up on Earth. He therefore saw no reason that Aristotelian science would

Nicholas Copernicus revolutionized astronomy by suggesting the Sun, not Earth, was at the center of the universe. *(Courtesy of the District Museum, Torun.)*

work in space. Galileo, though, had not yet publicly entered into the debate about how the planets, Sun, and Moon were arranged in the heavens, a controversy that began with the publication of Nicholas Copernicus's *On Revolutions of the Heavenly Spheres* in 1543.

The effort Galileo made to stay out of the debate about Copernicus during these years is uncharacteristic. In 1604, when a new star appeared in the sky and created a sensation, he made no comment. He knew that if the new star was located in the celestial sphere, Aristotle's theory of the unchanging heavens was invalid. He also knew that a new star had been discovered in 1572, which the Danish astronomer Tycho Brahe had studied. Brahe concluded the new star (actually it was a supernova— an exploding star) was located well beyond the Moon, but there were still skeptics. Galileo would have reason to disagree with other of Brahe's conclusions later in his career.

The 1604 star generated so much controversy, Galileo eventually had to address the subject in a public lecture. During the talk, he skillfully managed to avoid taking a stance by presenting all points of view on the issue.

German astronomer Johannes Kepler encouraged Galileo to publicly support the heliocentric theory of Nicholas Copernicus. *(Erich Lessing / Art Resource, NY.)*

There were hints that Galileo began doubting the Aristotelian model long before he used the telescope. The German Astronomer Johannes Kepler had sent him a copy of his first book, *Cosmological Mystery*, in 1597. Kepler was a young mathematics professor in present-day Austria. He was convinced that Copernicus was correct and had not hesitated to publicly endorse his ideas. Kepler was also a committed Pythagorean who believed that mathematics revealed as well as described nature. A few years younger than Galileo, Kepler was a deeply religious, even mystical man. He would later serve in the prestigious position of Imperial Mathematician at the court of the Holy Roman Emperor, even though the emperor was Catholic and Kepler was Protestant. *Cosmological Mystery* was the first work by a major astronomer that unquestioningly accepted Copernicus's theory and sought to promote a better understanding of the heliocentric system.

In his letter thanking Kepler for a copy of the book, Galileo wrote that he too thought Copernicus was right, but added, "I have preferred not to publish, intimidated by the fortune of our teacher Copernicus, who though he will be of immortal fame to some, is yet by an infinite number (for such is the multitude of fools) laughed at and rejected." This suggests he held back to avoid the ridicule of his fellow teachers and other academics. He wanted to wait for physical evidence to support the idea of a moving Earth before going public, and that evidence was not available before the invention of the telescope.

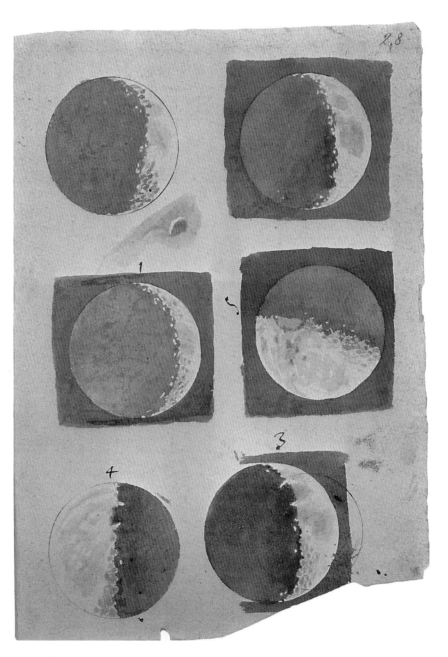

Galileo painted this watercolor of the Moon after viewing it through a telescope.
(Courtesy of the Biblioteca Nazionale Centrale, Florence, Italy.)

Galileo was probably the first human to consistently use a telescope in astronomy. After refining it to magnify distant objects approximately twenty times, he turned his attention to the Moon. Beginning in late November 1609, he followed Earth's satellite through its phases and made sketches and notes. What he saw was startling. The Moon was thought to be a flawless, smooth sphere, like a cue ball, but his observations revealed its surface to be "rough and uneven, and, just like the surface of the Earth itself, is everywhere full of vast protuberances, [and] deep chasms." On the Moon there were mountains and deep valleys and evidence of erosion.

After studying the Moon through December, he turned the telescope to distant Jupiter. He watched the planet nightly, steadying his hands and breath in order to stabilize the instrument. He made his most startling discovery when he detected first three, and then four, satellites circling the large planet. He made a series of observations and confirmed that the satellites, which he originally thought were stars, systematically changed position relative to Jupiter.

This meant Jupiter had moons, and this discovery dealt a huge blow to the theory of an Earth-centered universe. One pillar of geocentrism was the idea that all bodies orbited Earth. Secondly, and more profoundly, the anti-Copernicans had insisted that a moving Earth would speed away from the Moon. Because there was not yet an understanding of the attractive force of gravity, it seemed implausible that two bodies could orbit the

Sun in tandem. The smaller moon would certainly be left behind. Galileo, however, had discovered that Jupiter, which the Aristotelians said orbited the Earth, had four orbiting moons. How could a planet orbiting Earth have four moons, while it was considered impossible for Earth to circle the Sun with only one moon of its own?

Galileo was excited about his discoveries and wanted to make them public. He knew he would not be the only one to turn a telescope to the sky and did not want to lose credit for making the discoveries first.

While still observing Jupiter, Galileo began writing a sixty-page pamphlet he called *The Starry Messenger*. On March 13, 1610, a first edition of 550 copies was published. It sold out so fast he was only able to keep three copies for himself. Written in Latin, the accepted language for scholarship, the little book became a sensation throughout Europe. The British ambassador to the Venetian court sent a copy, along with a telescope, to King James I.

These were exciting years for astronomy. The process of validating Copernicus had begun. In Prague, Johannes Kepler had recently discovered, by use of mathematical analysis, that planetary orbits were elliptical, not circular, and that orbital speed varies de-

The title page of *Starry Messenger*, the book that made Galileo famous. *(Courtesy of University of Toronto, Fisher Rare Book Library.)*

pending on a planet's distance from the Sun. When he heard of Galileo's telescopic discoveries, he wrote him a letter of support. "Why should I not believe a most learned mathematician, whose very style attests the soundness of his judgement," the German wrote.

Galileo took advantage of his new celebrity to begin negotiating with the Medici family for a position in Florence. He had wanted to return home for years and was about to get his wish. To help his case, he named the moons of Jupiter the Medicean moons to honor the family, and dedicated *The Starry Messenger* to Cosimo II, the head of the family.

The flattery worked; Galileo got what he wanted. Cosimo made him mathematician to the Medici family and appointed him professor of philosophy and mathematics at the University of Pisa as well. To sweeten the offer, Galileo was not required to actually teach any classes, and he was paid a salary equal to what he had been granted by the Venetian senate. He was also promised a lifetime tenure with regular raises. Galileo was going home. At age forty-six, his discoveries with the telescope had made him the most respected, and notorious, scientist in Italy. His decision to leave his current position angered the Venetian senate, which had recently granted him a generous salary and placed large orders for his telescope. They saw his leave-taking as an act of ingratitude.

CHAPTER FOUR
PHASES OF VENUS

In late summer of 1610, after putting his affairs in order in Padua, Galileo, accompanied by his daughters, rode south to Florence. His son remained behind with his mother, but he would join his father a few years later. The move to Florence effectively ended Galileo's relationship with Marina, who later married a merchant and started a new family. The girls lived with Galileo's mother until they reached their teenage years, when he placed them both in convents, where they lived out their lives. He was apparently unwilling to arrange for their marriages, which would involve paying dowries to their husbands. When his son moved to Tuscany, he also lived with Galileo's mother until he went away to school.

Galileo spent most of his first months in Florence sick in bed. Florence is situated at a higher altitude than Venice and he had some difficulty adjusting to the thinner air. It is possible he still suffered from the effects of the waterfall gases to which he was exposed his first summer in Padua. "I have experienced the very thin air of Florence as a cruel enemy of my head and the rest of my body," he wrote a friend. He recuperated at the estate of Filippi Salviati, whose home was a gathering place for philosophers and other intellectuals and artists.

When he was first offered the chance to move back to Florence, several of his friends and supporters tried to convince him to stay in Venice, which had a stronger tradition of valuing academic freedom. He could not expect the same level of support from the Medici family.

The religious schism that had divided Europe since the beginning of the Protestant Reformation in 1517 grew increasingly tense in the early decades of the seventeenth century. What had started as a rebellion against the Catholic Church had now become an alternative version of Christianity that was itself splintering into a variety of different interpretations. In reaction to the spread of Protestantism, the Catholic Church had made internal reforms that came to be known as the Counter-Reformation. The Society of Jesus, or Jesuits, was a new order created by the Church to develop a better-educated clergy. Another aspect of the Counter-Reformation was the Inquisition, which was charged with ferreting out and prosecuting heretics and others

INQUISITION

There were actually three distinct Inquisitions. The first was organized by Pope Gregory IX in 1231 to find and try heretics. This was an era of religious uniformity, when deviation was considered to be a secular as well as religious threat. Heresy was a denial of Catholic teaching, and was punishable by death. Gregory also wanted to create a system of justice that would make the prosecution of heresy uniform. He was alarmed at the frequency of mob violence and the use of spurious charges of heresy as a way to destroy an enemy.

The inquisitors were taken primarily from the Franciscan and Dominican orders. They rode a circuit, much like judges in early America, and heard trials in specific areas.

The second Inquisition took place in Spain. It began in Castile in 1478 and was established to ferret out Jews and Muslims who had converted to Catholicism but were not "true believers." In 1483, the infamous Tomas de Torquemada took charge of the Spanish Inquisition. He established tribunals in the major cities to try the recent converts, or *Conversos*, many of whom were Catholic in name only. More than thirteen thousand *Conversos* were tried in the first twelve years of the Inquisition. Eventually, in 1492, the Jews were expelled from Spain in an attempt to stop contact between them and the recently converted.

The Roman Inquisition, which tried Galileo, was established in 1542 to resist the spread of Protestantism and to protect the faith from unorthodox beliefs, such as those preached by Giordano Bruno. In 1559 the Roman Inquisition drew up the first Index of Forbidden Books.

The College of Jesuits in Rome. *(Courtesy of the Gebinetto delle Stampe, Rome.)*

who presented ideas contrary to the accepted theology. The Inquisition gained power and influence at the Vatican as the struggle against Protestantism gained momentum.

As the Counter-Reformation increased in influence, the Vatican began an effort to exert more political control over the Italian peninsula. Venice resisted this pressure. At one point, the doge had even ordered all Jesuits and other Church officials to leave the republic. In 1607, tenuous peace was achieved when Pope Paul III agreed to stop pressuring the Venetians into submission.

The situation was quite different in Florence. Two members of the Medici family had served as pope, and in the Vatican's inner circle there was always a Medici cardinal, who was either a member of the family or a close ally. This relationship, combined with the more conservative intellectual traditions in Tuscany, as compared to Venice, is what prompted his friends to argue against Galileo's returning to Florence.

In 1610, though, an open conflict with the Church seemed remote. His principal opponents at the time were not the Jesuits, or the Inquisition, but the Peripatetics. Most of the Jesuits Galileo came into contact with were more open to Galileo's ideas than the Peripatetics were. While they could not openly endorse Copernicus, a great deal of Galileo's support among the educated elite at this stage of his career came from the Jesuits. Galileo considered himself to be a devout Christian who never questioned the truth of the Catholic Church's basic teachings. When he left Padua, he fully expected the Jesuits to continue their support of his scientific research. They would remain supportive, at least for a time.

He was beginning to need allies. Galileo's discoveries with the telescope intensified the opposition of the Aristotelians. Some of them refused to look through what they called the eye optick. Others presented arguments against its use. Among the criticisms were suggestions that the telescope made optical illusions appear to be real, placed objects in the sky that were not there, and created distortions with its magnifying power. They insisted that these flaws were responsible for the Moon's surface appearing craggy and pocked. The most personal attack was the assertion that the telescope appealed to men of low intelligence who were unsophisticated and unable to engage in philosophical discussions. Only a man of low order would stoop to peer through a mere device and accept what he thought he saw as truth. Was it any wonder, the Aristotelians said, that many of these same men also claimed Earth was in motion in defiance of their very own senses?

Galileo received a boost when Kepler, now in service to the Holy Roman Emperor Rudolph II, wrote a pamphlet supporting *The Starry Messenger*. Kepler had to wait months to find a telescope. As soon as he did, he confirmed both of Galileo's findings—the Moon's surface was not smooth, and Jupiter possessed its own moons.

Once his health had been restored, Galileo returned to his observations and immediately began to make new discoveries. He found what he thought were Saturn's two satellites. He was actually observing Saturn's rings, but his telescope was not powerful enough to let him make this distinction. His drawings of the planet, made in 1612, reveal how the images appeared to him.

When he turned his attention to Venus, Galileo made a discovery that convinced him the debate over Copernicus had been settled once and for all. Using his telescope, he began observing the planet Venus in the early evening hours during the autumn of 1610. Over a period of weeks, he watched the planet go through distinct phases. These phases proved that Venus orbited the Sun, just as the Moon's changing shape was a result of its orbiting Earth.

While Galileo's discovery of the phases of Venus proved it orbited the Sun, which certainly knocked the

This photo of the four Galilean moons of Jupiter was taken by the Hubble Space Telescope. Since Galileo's discovery, a total of 39 moons have been identified as satellites of Jupiter. *(NASA and The Hubble Heritage Team [STScII/AURA].)*

ground out from beneath Ptolemy's system of the heavens, another theory was available to explain the phases of Venus without having Earth move. Late in the sixteenth century, Tycho Brahe had proposed a planetary system in which the inner planets, Mercury and Venus, orbited the Sun. In turn, the Sun, along with the other planets, orbited Earth. Because Tycho's model had Venus orbiting the Sun with Earth remaining stationary, the phases of the second planet were explained in the context of geocentrism. This eventually became the favorite theory of those who did not accept Copernicus.

After discovering the phases of Venus, Galileo spent most of the year calculating the orbital periods of the moons of Jupiter. It took several months to arrive at accurate values of the moons' relative positions. He did this in preparation for a trip to Rome to present his telescopic discoveries at the Vatican and to others in the Holy City. Because he had named the moons of Jupiter after the Medici family, he wanted to know where each moon was at any given time, in case they were to be used in astrological charts. He hoped the presentation would bring glory to himself and to his Medici benefactors and strengthen his position in the struggle with the Aristotelians.

Galileo arrived in Rome on March 29, 1611. He planned to spend a great deal of time with his Jesuit friend and supporter Christoph Clavius, who directed the mathematics department at Roman College, the premier Jesuit school. Clavius was not a Copernican, but he had defended Galileo in lectures and debates. If he could appeal to Clavius's intellectual integrity, and impress him with his work on Jupiter, Venus, and the Moon, Galileo hoped he would be able to count on support from the highest Church officials.

Galileo demonstrated to Clavius and his colleagues how to use the telescope. He gave one to the Roman College so they could make their own observations.

PHASES OF VENUS

COPERNICUS   PTOLEMY

After hitting upon the idea that Venus cycled through phases, but before confirming his theory by tracking the planet through an entire cycle, Galileo sent Johannes Kepler word of his discovery buried in an anagram. He did this because he did not want to go public with an unproven hypothesis, but wanted proof that the discovery was his if someone else tried to claim priority. The translated anagram reads: "The Mother of Love [Venus was named after the Roman goddess of love] imitates the phases of the Moon." After observing Venus throughout December 1610, Galileo went public with his finding on New Year's Day, 1611.

The discovery of the phases of Venus dealt a mortal blow to Ptolemy's system, which had Venus, and the other planets, orbiting Earth on an epicycle moving on a deferent. In Ptolemy's model, it was impossible for Venus to go through the phases Galileo documented. However, the phases of Venus did not prove that the Copernican system was true. Late in the sixteenth century, the Danish astronomer Tycho Brahe devised a composite system in which all the planets, except Earth, revolved around the Sun, which in turn, orbited a central, stationary Earth. This system was geometrically interchangeable with that of Copernicus, but did not require a moving Earth, and for that reason became the preferred planetary model for many astronomers in the early seventeenth century.

While Clavius, who was in his seventies, still did not agree with Galileo that the phases of Venus proved Copernicus was right, he did confirm what Galileo saw. But there was no inherent conflict between Galileo and the Church, Clavius advised, as long as Galileo presented his arguments as a hypothesis. In other words, Galileo was on safe ground as long as he did not insist the phases of Venus, or any other discovery he made with the telescope, provided absolute proof of Copernican theory.

Clavius reported on his meeting with Galileo to Cardinal Bellarmino, a formidable and influential man who zealously defended the faith. In England, which became a Protestant nation in the sixteenth century, the cardinal was rumored to be the mastermind behind a notorious plot to blow up the Parliament. Protestant mothers all over Europe threatened, "Bellarmino will get you," as a way to keep their children in line. A powerful Jesuit, he was one of the most conservative prelates. Clavius reported to Bellarmino that Galileo's findings were not conclusive proof of Copernicus's theory, and they were being presented as a hypothesis only. This report smoothed the way for Galileo to be warmly received by Church officials.

On this trip, Galileo also met Cardinal Barberini for the first time. A trained mathematician, the Tuscan Barberini was a Medici cardinal. Galileo and Barberini enjoyed one another's company and had long discussions about science and literature. Although they had a

Cardinal Barberini, a fellow Tuscan, was an early ally of Galileo. *(Courtesy of Musée du Louvre.)*

cordial relationship, Galileo might have made the mistake of assuming Cardinal Barberini's friendship meant he agreed with him on astronomical matters.

Galileo was also the guest of Prince Federico Cesi, who had founded the Academy of the Lincei in 1603. The academy's mission was to study nature objectively without reference to earlier theories. The members shared Galileo's dedication to the experimental method. The group's name referred to the lynx, a feline animal that was legendary for its awareness of its surroundings and whose survival depended on its keen sight.

Cesi invited Galileo to join the Lincean Academy. He was only the second new member to be added since the group's beginning. Galileo's membership provided him with an influential forum to present his work, as well as a new circle of like-minded people with whom to discuss his ideas. The Linceans would publish several of his future books.

The 1611 visit to Rome was a huge success. Galileo was wined and dined and generally heralded as Italy's premier scientist. When he returned to Florence in the early summer, he had met with the most influential Jesuit philosophers and mathematicians and had received an audience with the pope. While most of the Vatican officials did not openly endorse his views, they did not attempt to stop him from writing or speaking on them either. To the contrary, he was encouraged to continue exploring the topic—as a scientific hypothesis.

Only a few years earlier, Galileo had been an obscure mathematician working in near solitude. At that time, his discoveries had been controversial among academics and intellectuals, but did not have the potential to lead to a public conflict with the Church. Since beginning to use the telescope, though, his life had entered a new phase. It had made him famous and relatively wealthy— and placed him at the heart of the debate over heliocentricism.

Before he used the telescope to discover physical evidence supporting Copernicus, he had apparently been willing to continue teaching Ptolemy to his students. It was characteristic of Galileo that he did not publicly advocate heliocentricism until he had visual evidence. Once he had what he considered to be conclusive proof, however, he was determined to convince everyone else he was right.

CHAPTER FIVE
BODIES IN WATER

One of Galileo's most persistent opponents was a professor named Ludovico delle Colombe. The two had first locked horns over the new star of 1604. After it had been sighted, Colombe printed a tract proposing it was not new but had simply not been visible before. An anonymous pamphlet ridiculing Colombe's thesis was published in 1606. Colombe suspected Galileo was the author—and he might have been, although that is not known for certain.

In 1610, when Galileo reported the surface of the Moon was craggy and rough, Colombe said Galileo's report might be accurate; it was what he saw through the telescope, but the surface he described was actually contained within a smooth, crystalline shell. In other words, the moon did have a covering of aether, as Aristotle had said. Colombe wrote to Clavius and offered his opinion about the Moon's surface. When Clavius asked Galileo to respond to Colombe's theory, Galileo wrote back that Colombe might be right, but how was one to know? "The hypothesis is pretty; its only fault is that it is neither demonstrated or demonstrable. Who does not see that this is a purely arbitrary fiction?"

After Galileo returned to Florence, a group led by Colombe began meeting to plan ways to undercut Galileo's reputation and support. They decided to engage him in public debates and displays. They hoped Galileo would slip up and anger someone who could do him harm, or make a public mistake that would embarrass him.

The first showdown was over hydrostatics, specifically, why ice floats on the surface of water. It began after a dinner, when Salviati, Galileo, and two Aristotelian professors were at Salviati's villa discussing what happens when water freezes. The Aristotelians chose the topic because they were convinced they were on solid scientific ground and that Galileo was sure to disagree with them. They hoped to prove their point and then force him to admit he was wrong in a public venue.

In the conversation, Colombe and the others held to the Aristotelian idea that ice was simply condensed water. Aristotle had stated that an element's form could not be altered. According to Aristotle, ice was merely frozen water, and because an element can never change its form, which included weight, water could not weigh any more, or less, frozen than it did unfrozen. So how did ice float if it did not weigh less than the water that supported it? The Aristotelians thought ice floated because of its shape, with the solid flat surface created by the freezing process making it possible for water to support it. They believed flotation was a product of shape, not weight.

Just as they had assumed he would, Galileo disagreed with their position. Ice, he said, was rarified water. Water did change its form when frozen—it became lighter. That was why ice floated, not because of its shape.

Less than a week after the discussion at Salviati's villa, Galileo received word that Colombe was making public demonstrations designed to prove Galileo wrong. Colombe had gathered pieces of ebony wood that were slightly denser than water. Some of the blocks were flat; others were in various shapes. In his demonstrations, Colombe pointed out the flat pieces floated, while the cylinders, spheres, and cone-shaped pieces sank. The only explanation for the difference was shape, he insisted, because they were all of equal weight.

Galileo thought he had no choice but to respond. The two men arranged to meet and settle the topic in a demonstration and debate. On the scheduled night, Colombe did not show up, and the controversy continued in letters and conversations. Galileo accepted every opportunity presented to publicly argue his position,

---

SURFACE TENSION

Water molecules have a cohesive force that creates surface tension. The water molecules at the surface are surrounded by like molecules beneath them, but not above them. This causes them to adhere more tightly to those that they have contact with. The stronger coherence creates a film across water, a tighter surface. It was this coherence of molecules, or surface tension, that Galileo discovered in his experiments recorded in *Bodies on Water*.

---

usually at dinner with his colleagues. Cardinal Barberini attended one such dinner and afterward wrote Galileo that he was very impressed with his argument regarding floating bodies. Galileo's joy was tempered, however, when he learned Cardinal Bellarmino supported Colombe.

Grand Duke Cosimo asked Galileo to stop performing at these public displays. He did not want his court mathematician acting like a circus monkey, he said. Galileo wrote the grand duke a long letter explaining the circumstances and his position. He promised to avoid any more of the public spectacles. He would address the question of floating bodies in a book-length manuscript. After a banquet attended by Barberini, held on October 2, 1611, Galileo withdrew to Salviati's villa and spent the winter writing this book.

The debate over hydrostatics returned Galileo yet again to principles first set out by Archimedes, who had determined that objects float because water exerts an upward thrust on the immersed object equal to the weight of the displaced water. When an object has a density the same as or less than the displaced water, it will float. When an object's density is greater, it will sink.

The problem Galileo addressed in *Bodies in Water* regarded why some objects with greater density than water, such as Colombe's ebony cones, floated. Colombe noted that when a cone was placed on the water with its pointed end up it floated. When it was placed in the water with its pointed end down, it sank. The density and element were consistent; the only thing different was the

Cardinal Bellarmino befriended Galileo but rejected the idea of a moving Earth as contrary to the scriptures. *(Courtesy of Instituto e Museo di Storia della Scienza, Florence, Italy.)*

Grand Duke Cosimo II was the ruler of
Tuscany and, also, Galileo's patron. He
cautioned him against entering into public
debates on questions about physics.
*(Courtesy of Instituto e Museo di Storia della
Scienza, Florence, Italy.)*

shape of the section of the cone that touched the water.
This led Colombe to conclude that flotation was a conse-
quence of shape.

Galileo conducted a series of experiments to observe
what happened when the cone was placed in the water.
He measured the amount of water displaced and discovered that the cone, when placed broad side down, created
a minute depression on the water's surface. The air in the
depression provided enough support to offset the cone's
density, allowing it to float. Conversely, when the cone

was placed in the water with the pointed end down, the depression created was so small that it would not allow enough air to gather and offset the cone's density at a level equal to the displaced water. The factor determining if an object will float, then, is the relative density of the object compared to water.

In *Bodies in Water*, Galileo's work with the cones essentially confirmed what Archimedes had written in the second century B.C. In that regard, it did not break new ground. His methodology, however, established a clear distinction between the way he approached science and the method Colombe employed. Galileo did not simply conduct a demonstration and make assumptions based on it. He proposed the most convincing argument on why bodies float, and then supported it with mathematical evidence. Surely, he thought, any fair-minded observer could see that.

Colombe and his supporters, however, were not inclined to be fair-minded; instead, they criticized the method Galileo used to conduct his experiments. Aristotle had said shape and matter were indivisible, and that it was improper to discuss an object's shape apart from its composition. In Colombe's opinion, Galileo had erred when he discussed the shape and weight of the submerged object without making reference to its composition. Furthermore, Galileo used wax cones weighted with lead in some of his experiments. Because Aristotle had said every object had a unique form, it was improper to compare an ebony cone to a wax cone filled with lead, even if their weight was the same.

Galileo aggravated the Peripatetics even more by writing *Bodies in Water* in Italian, instead of the Latin usually employed in scholarly publications. They saw it as a snub of their profession and their elite status in society. Galileo justified it by saying he knew thousands of workmen—shipbuilders, architects, engineers and others—who put mathematics and practical physics to work everyday. These "common people" would be able to use his book because it was written in their language. Only an academic, separated from the daily work of the average citizen, would cling to a principle that failed to match experience, he said, so why waste time with them. The natural world was his judge, not the professors.

The debate over floating bodies energized Galileo. In public lectures and letters, he intensified his attack on the practice of referring to dead authority figures to prove a point. He said those who favored rhetoric over quantitative analysis were afraid they would be proved wrong. The main purpose of the rhetorical method, he said, was to provide protection for academics who tried to solve problems they did not understand.

These were strong and insulting words directed toward proud and respected men. Galileo simply seemed unable to understand that everyone was not as eager to embrace change as he was. He was certainly not interested in slowing down to wait for them. He knew he was at the peak of his powers, and he was determined to push into the future while he still had the energy.

CHAPTER SIX
SUNSPOTS

Early in 1612, Galileo received a pamphlet from Mark Welser, an amateur scientist who lived in southern Germany. Welser asked Galileo to give his opinion on some spots the pamphlet writer, who called himself Apelles, claimed to have discovered the previous May while viewing the Sun through a telescope.

Welser informed Galileo that Apelles was actually the well-known Jesuit astronomer Father Christoph Scheiner, who taught mathematics at a university in Germany. Scheiner had developed a way to observe the Sun indirectly by allowing its image to pass through a telescope onto a card. Scheiner used the technique to make several observations. He had confirmed the existence of black spots on or near the Sun's surface. In his pamphlet, Scheiner speculated the spots were either on the surface of the Sun itself, or they were closely orbiting planets. Scheiner, as a Jesuit, settled on the side of the spots being orbiting planets. He said they were similar to the satellites of Jupiter that Galileo had discovered.

Galileo rejected Scheiner's conclusion that the spots were planets. Scheiner's use of *The Starry Messenger* to support his thesis did not make Galileo happy, either. The theory was based on weak reasoning, and he did not want his most famous work used to justify it.

In his first letter to Welser, Galileo insisted that he had seen the sunspots months before Scheiner. He said he

Christoph Scheiner built a device similar to this to make observations of sunspots.
(From Christopher Scheiner: Rosa Ursina, *1630.)*

had even shown them to people while visiting Rome. Although his busy schedule had not allowed him to write on the subject yet, he said these witnesses would support him in his claim of having made the discovery first. Galileo then went on to methodically undercut Scheiner's satellite theory.

Galileo wrote three long letters on sunspots. They were addressed to Welser but were intended for publication. He began the first by apologizing for the delay in writing. It had been three months since he had received the pamphlet. "I . . . must be more cautious," he wrote, "than most other people in pronouncing upon anything new . . . Even the most trivial error is charged to me as a capital fault by the enemies of innovations."

Scheiner thought the spots were planets drawn along by the Sun's rotation. If that was true, Galileo said, they would be as predictable as the moons of Earth or Jupiter. Clearly, the sunspots were far too unpredictable to be orbiting satellites. Galileo also pointed out the spots enlarged and decayed into irregular shapes in unpredictable periods. No satellite behaved this way.

The spots were clearly not satellites, he concluded. Furthermore, they indicated the Sun was not stationary, but spun on its axis. He determined this by selecting a single point of the Sun's surface and observing and recording its changes for a month. As he made his observations, he saw the spots were of various sizes, and some were visible longer than others. He followed a single spot as it appeared on one edge of the Sun, slipping into view as though it were emerging from the backside of a sphere. The spot then began to grow wider—as though bulging outward—as it traveled over the central part of the disc. In its final stage, the spot shortened and began to disappear around the opposite side. This convinced him the spot was on the face of the Sun, and that the Sun rotated. He concluded by saying the spots were analogous to the clouds in Earth's atmosphere. Clouds appear and disappear, change shape and size, and would track closely to the face of Earth if viewed from such a distance.

Galileo wrote his final letter to refute a second pamphlet Scheiner had written in response to Galileo's criticism. Galileo sent all three letters to Prince Cesi, who convinced the Lincean Academy to publish them. The *Letters on Sunspots* were published, in Italian, in 1613. Although Galileo never referred to Scheiner by name in the letters—he always referred to the author of the original pamphlet as "Apelles"—the author's real identity was a well-known fact.

Letters on Sunspots created a sensation. Its thesis and conclusions were based on close observation, and were reasoned with remarkable clarity. Even the stubborn Aristotelians, who were essentially immune to most evidence presented by Galileo at this point, had to admit Scheiner's ideas were unsupportable. Galileo had again bested an upholder of the Aristotelian orthodoxy. Unfortunately, this time the Aristotelian was also an influential member of the Jesuits, a group which had tended

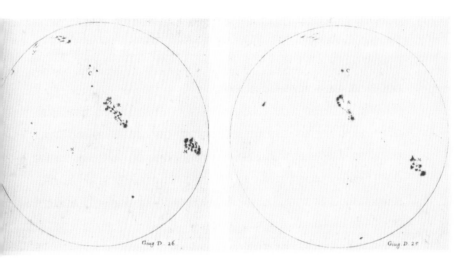

Galileo made this drawing of spots moving across the face of the Sun.
(Courtesy of the Royal Astronomical Society, London.)

to support Galileo in the past. The publication of *Letters on Sunspots* caused a strain in the previously cordial relationship he had enjoyed with the Society of Jesus.

During this debate over sunspots, Galileo made his first conclusive pro-Copernican public statement. In the first letter, discussing the method he had used to calculate the phases of Venus two years before, he wrote: "With absolute necessity we shall conclude, in agreement with the theories of the Pythagoreans and of Copernicus, that Venus revolves around the Sun just as do all the other planets." Now he was, for better or worse, a public advocate of the Copernican position. By making this declaration in a letter refuting a Jesuit scholar, Galileo had, intentionally or not, thrown down a challenge to those in the Church who saw the idea of a moving Earth as contrary to scripture. He had also opened himself up to attack from Colombe and others. If they could align the Church against Galileo, they might receive through official sanction what they could not win in scientific debate.

While *Letters on Sunspots* was published in Rome to a great deal of enthusiasm and debate, Galileo was revising *Bodies in Water*. He added more experimental data. This confluence of two controversial books launched a storm of publications in support of, and in opposition to, Galileo's work.

In the midst of the controversy, Galileo wrote to Cardinal Carlo Conti, a personal friend, about the Church's position regarding the possibility of change occurring in the celestial sphere. The cardinal assured him that the Church held no official position on Copernicus so far, but that Galileo should still tread cautiously when discussing a moving Earth and central Sun. Conti suggested that maybe someday the passage in the Bible which referred to the Sun standing still could be reconciled with Copernicus, possibly by proposing that the Bible had been written so it could be understood by the uneducated as well as the educated. But the time was not yet right for that argument.

His letter to Cardinal Conti was a turning point in Galielo's career. Before, he had challenged professors and philosophers and created controversy with his insistentence on the use of the scientific method, but he was still operating in the relatively narrow world of the educated elite then, where he was on solid ground.

Now he was about to enter the much more dangerous world of religious belief and the politics around it. He had come to believe there was no conflict between Copernicus and the teachings of the Church. He thought that God had explained the spiritual in the scriptures, which was the domain of the Church. To understand the natural world, God had given us minds, with which we could study and evaluate it.

Galileo wanted the Church to side with him on the proposition that is was possible to be both a good Catholic and a Copernican. This goal, however, thrust him directly into the ultimate rhetorical debate, of exactly the type he usually avoided, where the ancient authority called upon was nothing less than Holy Scripture. Furthermore, he was trying to force the most powerful institution in Italy to change.

In retrospect, while it can be argued that entering into this fight might not have been the wisest course of action for Galileo to pursue, by 1612 he might have felt he had no choice. He had already begun to hear rumors about a developing partnership between his philosophical enemies and some members of the clergy. A friend from Rome wrote him:

> A certain crowd of ill-disposed men envious of your virtue and merits met at the house of the archbishop there [in Florence] and put their heads together in a mad quest for any means by which they could damage you, either with regard to the motion of the Earth or otherwise. One of them wished to have a preacher

state from the pulpit that you were asserting outlandish things . . . I write this to you so that your eyes will be open to such envy and malice on the part of that sort of evildoers.

Colombe, whose name means "dove" in Italian, and whose followers were dubbed "The Pigeons" by Galileo, realized after reading *Letters on Sunspots* that the best way to silence Galileo was to focus on his belief in a moving Earth. The Catholic Church, locked in its long struggle with the Protestant Reformation, was growing increasingly impatient with any doctrine or idea that threatened its stability. It was not a good time to challenge some of the basic assumptions of the faith. To insist the Earth moved, and that this idea would not do damage to the central tenets of the faith, was exactly the sort of thing that could move the Church to retaliate.

A dramatic change had occurred in the cultural and intellectual environment over the last seventy-five years. In 1543, when the Catholic canon Nicholas Copernicus published *On Revolutions of the Heavenly Spheres*, he dedicated it to Pope Paul III, the pope who launched the Counter-Reformation. In 1532, ten years before the full text was published, but after its ideas had been summarized in a short pamphlet, the pope's personal secretary gave a lecture, delivered in a garden at the Vatican, in support of Copernicus's heliocentric theory.

In Copernicus's time, and for decades afterward, there was little concern that a central Sun and a moving Earth would conflict with Catholic theology. Although he was Protestant, the Copernican Johannes Kepler did most of his work while on the payroll of the Catholic Holy Roman emperor.

Nearly fifty years after the publication of Copernicus's book, the experience of Giordano Bruno's short life marked a watershed in the Catholic Church's attitude toward heliocentricism. Sixteen years older than Galileo, Bruno began his career as a monk in the Dominican order, but soon became disenchanted with corruption within the Church. Charged with heresy and excommunicated, he left Italy and for the next few years traveled Europe advocating a return to what he called an earlier version of Christianity. During his travels, probably while in England, he became a Copernican because he thought the Sun-centered theory suggested the possibility of an infinite universe. Bruno believed there were other planets populated with God's creatures, and this idea became the primary theme in his public sermons and writings. He returned to Italy in 1591, apparently convinced he could convert the pope to his ideas. Instead, he was arrested, tried by the Inquisition, and burned at the stake.

Although Galileo was not a religious figure and posed no direct threat to Catholic theology, Bruno's experience affected anyone who publicly advocated heliocentricism. The example of Bruno was often raised when Galileo's friends tried to talk him out of entering into theological discussions. They pointed out there was little danger of religious persecution if he kept his arguments on the scientific or hypothetical level. They implored him to leave the theology to the priests. Galileo, however, was convinced the Church had to accept his premise that there was no inherent contradiction between Copernicus and the Bible.

The first round in this new conflict began in 1613 at a banquet at the Medici summer palace in Pisa, when the grand duke's mother, Grand Duchess Cristina, questioned one of Galileo's allies and former students, Benedetto Castelli. The grand duchess surprised her guests when she suddenly remarked that Cosimo Boscaglia, a professor at the University of Pisa, had told her of Castelli and Galileo's adherence to the Copernican theory. Boscaglia, a friend of Colombe's, had also said Copernicus was contrary to the Holy Scriptures. What did Castelli have to say to this charge?

Boscaglia and Colombe had picked their instrument of attack well. Grand Duchess Cristina was a religious

Giordano Bruno was burned at the stake for preaching that Copernicus was not contrary to Christian theology. *(Courtesy of the British Museum.)*

enthusiast who was very conservative on matters of faith. The mother of Galileo's patron, there was no one in all of Italy who better combined access to great power with religious fervor.

Castelli did his best to convince the Grand Duchess there was no conflict between Copernicus and the faith. When the night was over, Castelli was convinced he had won the argument because Boscaglia had not attempted to refute his points. But Castelli failed to grasp the importance of what had happened. Boscaglia's goal was not to win a public argument, but to find a way to have the question entered into public discourse at a level so elevated it could not be ignored.

Galileo immediately saw the danger Castelli failed to detect. He began a long letter that was later released as *A Letter to Grand Duchess Cristina*. He hoped to nip the controversy in the bud, but it might have been better to simply not have responded. By answering the grand duchess, he sank even deeper into a theological argument and began fighting his enemies on their terms.

Galileo argued in the letter that the passages in the Bible conflicting with Copernicus were literary devices intended to speak to the common reader. The biblical reference most often used to dispute Copernicus was from the Book of Joshua and describes how God made the Sun stand still to lengthen the day in order to give the Israelites time to destroy their enemies. Galileo pointed out that this passage was actually more in harmony with Copernicus than with Aristotle. In Aristotle's

Grand Duchess Cristina, the mother of Galileo's patron, challenged the idea that a moving Earth did not conflict with scripture and led the movement against Copernicus's work by the Roman Inquisition.

cosmology, the entire heavens would have stopped. If Copernicus were right, only the Sun and Earth would have been held motionless.

Galileo went on to offer his opinion that there was no conflict between nature and religion. He observed, measured, and reported on what he found in the physical world, by use of the gifts God had given him. The Bible was God's way of explaining the spiritual world. The problem, he concluded, was not due to an inherent conflict between religion and science. It came from those who were driven to misuse religion because they were incapable of understanding the natural world.

It was a brilliant performance. The letter was passed around among supporters and enemies. Castelli was convinced its irrefutable logic would end the effort to portray Galileo as an enemy of the Church. Galileo also seemed to think he had put the matter to rest. He returned to work trying to predict the orbits of Jupiter's moons.

The tension between Galileo and the Church was too deeply rooted to simply dissolve, though. After a year of relative tranquility, new events took Galileo by surprise and raised the conflict to an even higher level.

On Sunday morning, December 21, 1614, a Dominican named Tommaso Caccini delivered a blistering attack against Galileo and his fellow mathematicians from the pulpit of his Church in Florence. Caccini accused mathematicians of doing the work of the devil and suggested the idea of a moving Earth was heresy. Caccini's sermon created a firestorm.

Galileo's devoted friend, Benedetto Castelli, mistakenly thought he had convinced Grand Duchess Cristina that there was no conflict between Copernicus and Christianity.
(Courtesy of Instituto e Museo di Storia della Scienza, Florence, Italy.)

The Pigeons had finally found a clergyman willing to attack the famous Galileo from the pulpit. Castelli wrote him that he was afraid the roar of public condemnation created by the sermon would drive the study of science and mathematics out of the University of Pisa. Because the monk had stirred up such an outpouring from the citizenry, it would be best for everyone if Galileo remained home and concentrated on his work in physics and refused to even discuss astronomy. Their best strategy was to wait, Castelli said. Cesi wrote from Rome and reminded Galileo he had once heard Cardinal Barberini, whom Galileo considered to be a friend, say a moving Earth was contrary to scripture. Cesi agreed with Castelli that the best they could hope for at this dangerous time was to stop the attacks on mathematics. There was no chance of advancing the cause of Copernicus.

This was a wise strategy, but it was one Galileo was incapable of following. Deeply troubled by the public reaction to the sermon, he decided it was time to return to Rome and make his case before the cardinals. Going to the Holy City had worked for Galileo before, so he hoped it would work again this time around.

CHAPTER SEVEN
DEFEAT IN ROME

Before he left for Rome, Galileo sent Cardinal Barberini a copy of the letter he had written to Grand Duchess Cristina. Barberini's response was an omen of things to come: Did not Psalm nineteen specifically mention the Sun's movement? he asked. How did Galileo reconcile this passage with Copernicus?

It must have been clear at this point that this trip to Rome would be more difficult than the visit in 1611, but Galileo was convinced of his great power of persuasion. He was determined to continue repeating his basic premise—that there was no conflict between Copernicus and the Holy Scriptures—until, at last, it was accepted. The only conflict, he said in response to Cardinal Barberini, was due to the limitations of his enemies.

Galileo left for Rome in early December 1615. He had arranged to stay at the Tuscan Embassy, as befitted his official position. Cardinal Barberini advised him to avoid discussing Copernicus and the Bible together when meeting with Church officials. He should concentrate on Copernicus and limit his comments to the scientific evidence. To say the Bible was written to be understood by the common people and could not be relied upon for scientific truth would anger the Inquisition cardinals by its suggestion that scripture was less profound than mathematics and astronomy.

Publicly, Galileo's initial reception in Rome was positive. He was the guest of honor at several banquets and maintained an active agenda. He also spent hours developing his theory that the ocean tides proved Earth's motion. This argument is today considered to be one of his biggest mistakes.

Galileo first conceived the idea that tides were the result of Earth's motion in 1595, while traveling on a barge carrying fresh water into Venice. As the barge turned he watched the water slosh and bounce. When the barge slowed, he noticed that the sloshing diminished at a steady pace.

Wouldn't Earth's two motions, orbiting the Sun and rotating on its axis, create a similar effect on the oceans? He pondered and worked on the idea for years. Now, as he began to enter into a debate with the Inquisition over the theory of a moving Earth, he wrote a short treatise arguing that the tides were a result of Earth's motion.

The title page of the first edition of Nicholas Copernicus's book, *On the Revolutions of the Heavenly Spheres,* first published in 1543, in Nuremberg, Germany.

Today we know the tides are caused by the tug of the Moon's gravity, but Galileo believed his thesis provided a persuasive argument in favor of Copernicus.

Galileo's primary goal was to keep Copernicus's book, *On the Revolutions of the Heavenly Spheres,* off the index of suspended books, which would forbid Catholics from reading it. Secondly, he hoped to use his tide theory to convince the cardinals that the physical evidence for a moving Earth was overwhelming.

Some of Galileo's supporters argued for a different strategy. Instead of increasing the pressure on the Church with his tide theory, it might be wiser to find a way to *reduce* pressure. His enemies had dragged the Church into the conflict. If Galileo argued that Copernicus's model could not be proven absolutely and should continue to be treated as a hypothesis as it had been since 1543, it could be possible to avoid an open conflict. Furthermore, it would expose the Pigeon League and its supporters within the Church as the instigators of the trouble. Galileo, however, was determined to win over the cardinals to his view.

Galileo's campaign to convince the Catholic Church of his ideas started off badly and got worse. When his theory of the tides was mentioned to Pope Paul V as proof of a moving Earth, the pope became agitated. God could move the tides any way he wished, the pontiff snapped. He then demanded the Inquisition settle once and for all the entire question of Earth's motion. Pope Paul V was not an intellectual and was said to despise men of letters. In his presence, the Jesuits around him often tried to appear less learned than they were. But Pope Paul V had other reasons for being in a bad mood. His reign was filled with conflicts with Venice and other Italian republics, as well as increasing tensions with the Protestants in Central Europe. The Church's authority was being attacked on all fronts, and he had little patience for conflicts between scholars and theologians over an astronomical theory.

When he heard of the pope's outburst, Galileo saw the writing on the wall. He knew that, without strong papal and Jesuit support for his ideas, the Inquisition would surely rule against him. His only hope had been to gather enough support to intimidate the cardinals who ran the Inquisition into not taking a position on the question.

Now it was clear this was not going to happen. When it was made public that the question of whether Copernicus's theory was heretical had been turned over to the Inquisition, Galileo's invitations to banquets and requests for lectures dried up.

In February 1616, Cardinal Bellarmino, who respected Galileo but was a supporter of the Pigeon League, discussed how the Inquisition's inquiry should proceed. It was decided they would not even consider the scientific and mathematical validity of the question. This was not their concern. The Inquisition would only look at two propositions made by Copernicus and determine if they were in conflict with Church teachings:

1. The Sun is the center of the universe, and is therefore immobile.
2. The Earth is not the center of the universe, nor is it motionless, but moves with a whole (annual) and daily motion.

To no one's surprise, the first proposition was found to be heretical to scripture and "foolish and absurd" as well. The second proposition was also determined to be "bad" philosophy and "erroneous in faith."

The Inquisition's decision was made on February 23, 1616. Two days later, the pope ordered Cardinal Bellarmino to officially inform Galileo of the decision and to warn him against expressing his opinion that there was no conflict between Copernicus and scripture.

The next day, two officials from the Inquisition es-

Pope Paul V, who was said to despise intellectuals, ordered the Inquisition cardinals to decide if Copernicus's book was heretical. *(Courtesy of Alinari.)*

corted Galileo from the Florentine Embassy to Cardinal Bellarmino's office. Galileo was then informed that *On Revolutions of the Heavenly Spheres* would be placed on index, which meant that Catholics were forbidden to read the book until it had been "corrected." Furthermore, Galileo was not to write or teach Copernicus's ideas as absolute truth, or to present the argument that the scriptures were not authoritative on matters of science.

Although this was not quite the turn of events Galileo had hoped for, it was not as bad as it could have been, either. Copernicus's book was not condemned, it was merely suspended. Also, Galileo himself was not specifically mentioned in the decree, and none of his own works were declared suspended or condemned.

Galileo had an audience with Pope Paul V on March 11, 1616. The pope expressed respect for Galileo and assured him that he held him in the highest esteem.

Galileo's opponents in Pisa and Florence were not satisfied with this outcome. They had hoped to have Galileo permanently silenced and his works banned. They began to spread the story that Galileo had been forced to denounce Copernicus and to offer up penance for his scientific ideas. Hearing of these rumors, Galileo asked Bellarmino to write a letter clearing his name and stating that he had not been punished while in Rome. The cardinal conceded to write a letter clarifying that Galileo had not been punished or forbidden from discussing Copernicus as a hypothesis, although he went on to say the belief that "the Earth moves around the Sun and that the Sun stands still in the center of the universe without motion from east to west is contrary to Sacred Scripture."

With this signed letter in hand, a somewhat vindicated Galileo returned to Florence. He had failed to convince the leaders of the Church that there was no inherent conflict between Copernicus and Catholic theology. He had not been condemned, but he had been ordered to stop speaking and writing about heliocentricism as more than a hypothesis. Maybe in the future, when the political climate changed, the issue could be revisited. In the meantime, there were many other scientific questions to investigate.

CHAPTER EIGHT
ASSAYER

Galileo's enemies among the Jesuits were frustrated that he did not receive a tougher sanction. They might have even resorted to forgery. After his meeting with Bellarmino, an unsigned addition was added to the official citation in Galileo's file in the Vatican. It read:

> In the palace and residence of Cardinal Bellarmino
> . . . the Cardinal admonished Galileo . . . that the
> opinion that the Sun is in the center of the universe and
> the Earth moves must be entirely abandoned, nor
> might he from then on in any way hold, teach, or
> defend it by word or in writing; otherwise the Holy
> Office would proceed against him.

This statement differed from the official decree Galileo

had been shown and also from the letter Bellarmino gave him. There is still considerable debate regarding the origin, and Galileo's awareness, of this second, more severe injunction. It might have been drawn up to be presented to Galileo if he refused to accept the terms of the first decree Bellarmino presented to him. When he did not offer any overt resistance to the decree, seeming to meekly accept the decision of the Inquistion, the harsher statement could have been filed away without Galileo ever having been made aware of its existence.

It is also possible that Galileo knew of the second document and may have even been served with it, but once he had the less restrictive letter from Bellarmino he decided to pretend the other injunction did not exist. As far as Galileo understood it, then, so long as he did not argue as absolute truth that Earth moved, or that Copernicus had not conflicted with scripture, he would not be persecuted. But the document in question clearly states that Galileo was told to "entirely abandon" Copernican theory and not even to address it as a hypothesis. Furthermore, he was forbidden to teach the idea at all. This was a major difference, and one that would be critical in Galileo's next, more dangerous conflict with the Inquistion.

The Pigeon League and their Jesuit supporters, led by Christopher Scheiner, the German Jesuit who nursed a grudge against Galileo because of the sunspots debate, might have reasoned it would only be a matter of time before Galileo would be compelled to speak or write again on the issue of a moving Earth and central Sun. They were willing to be patient, but wanted to make certain Galileo's next run-in with the Inquisition would have more serious consequences.

From this point on, the Jesuits were Galileo's most powerful opponents. He had antagonized many of them with his *Letters on Sunspots*, and, on a personal level, he was seen as intellectually arrogant. Another more political issue was that conservative members of the order had always opposed Copernicus on religious grounds. After the 1616 ruling, those Jesuits who had been inclined to accept Copernicus's ideas found themselves in a difficult situation. Many tried to obscure their earlier support by joining the anti-Galileo faction.

Galileo attempted to keep a low profile after his visit to Rome in 1615, and began work on less controversial matters. In one project, he sought to find a way to use the orbits of the moons of Jupiter to find longitude at sea. This problem had long hindered international trade, as navigators needed to know the ship's location at all times. Latitude, the ship's position north or south of the equator, could be obtained by measuring the altitude of the Sun or the Moon. To arrive at a correct longitude, though, one needed to know the exact time at the place from which the longitude was being measured, and accurate ship clocks would not exist for another century.

Galileo discovered that Jupiter's moons went into eclipse on a regular schedule. If he could compute charts of these eclipses, navigators could use the moons like a clock. Unfortunately, using a telescope on a ship was nearly impossible because the water's motion made it difficult to hold the telescope steady enough to view Jupiter's moons. Galileo worked on attaching a telescope with two eyepieces to a helmet. This was an advancement over earlier attempts but, in the end, the problem of making accurate astronomical observations from a ship was insurmountable and the project was abandoned.

Although Galileo tried to avoid open conflict with the Church, he did not pretend to have altered his Copernican views. In May 1618, he sent copies of his books *Letters on Sunspots* and *Treatise on the Tides* to several people. Both books made clear his commitment to heliocentricism as a hypothesis, though he added the following disclaimer:

> Now, since I know how necessary it is to obey and believe in the decisions of the superiors, as men who are led by higher knowledge which my humble mind cannot attain by itself, I regard this present essay which I am sending you—founded on the earth's mobility, and being one of the physical arguments which I produced in confirmation of that mobility— I repute this, I say, as a bit of poetry, or a dream.

In April 1617, Galileo moved to a rented villa called Bellosguardo, built on a hillside overlooking Florence. He sold the crops grown on the land to help pay the rent. Suffering from illness most of that winter, he was confined to bed until spring, when he made a pilgrimage to a religious shrine on the Adriatic coast, returning home in June. His son, Vincenzio, was now living with him, and two students boarded at the villa also. The rent students paid, and the fees Galileo earned from tutoring, brought in needed money. Then, in September 1618, just as the students completed their stay, he took sick yet again.

These recurring bouts of illness might have been malaria or typhoid, or may have been the result of a rheumatic problem. He had a kidney ailment, which is often associated with gout. He enjoyed drinking wine, sometimes to excess, and this no doubt aggravated his problem. He still suffered from exposure to the gases at the waterfall in Padua when he was a young man. It was around this time that he also began to have problems

This is an illustration of a comet that appeared in 1587. *(Courtesy of the Department of Prints and Drawings of the Zentralibibliothek, Zurich.)*

with his eyes. "As a result of a certain affliction I began to see a luminous halo more than two feet in diameter around the flame of a candle, capable of concealing from me all objects which lay behind it," he explained to a friend. He added, "As my malady diminished, so did the size and density of this halo."

Galileo apparently tried to use his eye problems to avoid making comments on the comets that startled Europe in the fall of 1618. The first one appeared in September; there were two more in November. Comets were traditionally interpreted as omens, and many concluded these comets indicated God's displeasure at the Thirty Years' War, which had recently begun in Central Europe between Protestants and Catholics.

These were the first comets to appear since the inven-

Danish astronomer Tycho Brahe studied the 1577 comet and determined that it intersected planetary orbits, which was contrary to the philosophy of Aristotle and Ptolemy. *(Courtesy of The Royal Library, Copenhagen.)*

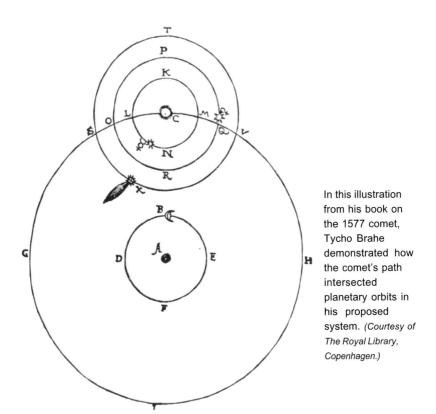

In this illustration from his book on the 1577 comet, Tycho Brahe demonstrated how the comet's path intersected planetary orbits in his proposed system. *(Courtesy of The Royal Library, Copenhagen.)*

tion of the telescope, and it is hard to believe that Galileo, the first man to have turned the telescope to the heavens, resisted the urge to observe them. When asked his opinion of their appearance, though, he claimed illness had kept him inside.

Galileo maintained his silence on the comets until he received a copy of a pamphlet rushed into print about their appearance. The author of the pamphlet was said to be Orazio Grassi, but Galileo thought it was the work of a committee of Jesuits who had met in Rome that fall.

EDMOND HALLEY AND THE COMET

Edmond Halley (1656-1742) was the son of a businessman who lost most of his wealth in the great London fire of 1666. This financial setback meant that Halley was taught at home until he entered St. Paul's School as a teenager. At St. Paul's, Halley was soon recognized to be a brilliant student, particularly in mathematics and astronomy. It was said of the young man that if a star were misplaced in the heavens, he would discover it.

Halley entered Queens College at Oxford in 1673. In 1675, while still a student, he went to work with John Flamsteed, the first Astronomer Royal, where he made observations of Mars. He left Oxford in 1676 without a degree and traveled to the island of St. Helena to map the stars in the Southern Hemisphere. He remained on the island for eighteen months. When he returned to England in 1678, he published his star catalog and was elected to the Royal Society of Science at age twenty-two.

Over the next few years, he was very active in the Royal Society. In 1684, he called on Isaac Newton, at the time a professor of mathematics at Cambridge, to discuss what type of gravitational force would produce an elliptical orbit. He was surprised to discover Newton had already worked out the proofs but did not seem inclined to publish his findings. Halley encouraged him to do so. Later, he encouraged Newton to publish his masterwork, *Principia Mathematica*. When the Royal Society could not come up with the funds to pay for the printing, Halley advanced the money from his own pocket, although he was not a wealthy man.

Halley first became intrigued with comets as a young man, when he observed one while returning from a trip to the Southern Hemisphere. Back in Europe, he rushed to Paris to meet with Jean-Dominique Cassini, who had gained fame by discovering four of Saturn's moons. Cassini had observed the comet in Paris and thought it was the same one that had appeared in 1577 and was written about by the Danish astronomer Tycho Brahe. Halley was intrigued with the idea that comets might follow a regular orbit.

Although Newton argued for parabolic orbits, Halley was convinced the elliptical orbits of planets also applied to comets. When another comet appeared in 1682, he compared it to earlier observations and found it to be similar to the one that had appeared in the years 1531 and 1607. He also found that the orbital pattern was elliptical. Halley predicted that the 1682 comet would reappear in December 1758 and, though he did not live to see it, the comet that now bears his name showed up right on schedule.

During the remainder of Halley's life, he worked on finding a method to determine longitude at sea, investigated tides and currents, and made more astronomical observations. In 1704, he became a professor of mathematics at Oxford, where he studied the motions of stars and entered into various scientific controversies, often in support of Newton. In 1720 he succeeded John Flamsteed to become the second Astronomer Royal.

There had also been a series of public speeches in which Grassi had given the Jesuits' opinion on the comets.

The pamphlet agreed with Tycho Brahe's book on the 1577 comet. Tycho, Europe's most accomplished observer prior to the telescope, had determined that comets traveled beyond the Moon in Aristotle's supposedly immutable celestial sphere. He had also said the 1577 comet orbited the Sun and its path intersected planetary orbits, which would have been impossible if the planets traveled in crystalline spheres.

Galileo was convinced that the Jesuits had been motivated to accept Tycho's conclusions on comets for another reason. As mentioned earlier, Tycho, who had rejected both Ptolemy and Copernicus's planetary models, had developed his own scheme that maintained a central, stationary Earth, but allowed for relative motion by having the Sun and Moon orbit Earth, and the other planets orbit the Sun. Tycho's hybrid structure became more popular after Galileo's discovery of the phases of Venus, which was the first conclusive physical evidence that a planet orbited the Sun. Placing the planets in motion around the Sun, and the Sun in motion around Earth, had created a system that explained the phases of Venus without requiring a moving Earth. In effect, by supporting Tycho's position on the comets, the Jesuits were preparing the way to replace Ptolemy's planetary model with Tycho's because it upheld a stationary Earth.

There was no physical evidence that could be used to discredit Tycho's system. It was possible, though, to point out errors in the reasoning of its supporters. Soon after the appearance of Grassi's pamphlet, Galileo's former student Mario Guiducci was elected as a consul of the prestigious Florentine Academy. This honor required him to make an inaugural address. Galileo decided to use the occasion to turn Guiducci into his spokesman. Together they wrote an address eventually titled *Discourse on the Comets.*

Grassi had said the comet, which he observed through a telescope, showed a small parallax. He interpreted this to mean the comet was very far away.

Galileo replied that it was ridiculous to attempt to use a telescope to measure distance. It was also a mistake to use parallax to locate a comet because there was not enough known about them. He went on to say that Grassi should not have accepted what Tycho had written about comets because so little was known about them. No one knew, for instance, if comets were in the celestial sphere or if they orbited the Sun. It was even possible that they could be restrained to the upper reaches of Earth's atmosphere. He wrote that comets might even be immaterial, "anomalous illuminations in the air." Or they might merely be illuminated parts of larger vaporous clouds, much like rainbows. Fundamentally, Galileo argued that no one really knew what comets were or how they behaved and that it was foolish to claim differently.

No one was fooled by Guiducci's name on the title page of *Discourse on the Comets*. Grassi and the Jesuits, who hoped Galileo had been silenced by the 1616 decision, reacted by composing another pamphlet entitled *The Astronomical Balance: Weighing Galileo's Opinions on Comets*. By addressing Galileo directly, they made it clear they did not believe Guiducci had written *Discourse*. *The Astronomical Balance* was published under the name Sarsi, who was one of Grassi's former students, as another way of letting Galileo know they were on to his game of hiding behind his former student.

The Astronomical Balance was an angry and open attack on Galileo couched in scientific language. Its real intent was to discuss the issues of comets and Tycho's system in light of the Church's recent condemnation of Copernicus. Maybe they could taunt Galileo into responding in a way that violated the decree:

> But suppose we grant that my master [Grassi] followed
> Tycho. How much of a crime is that? Whom might he
> follow instead? Ptolemy? Or Copernicus? All who
> are dutiful will call everyone away from him, and
> reject and spurn his recently condemned hypothesis.

The message was clear. Galileo should remain silent on astronomical questions or risk the wrath of the Church.

Although his friends at the Lincean Academy encouraged him to respond quickly to *The Astronomical Balance*, Galileo spent two years composing his response. He knew he could not even mention the name Copernicus. At the same time, though, he wanted to state his scientific philosophy clearly.

When the work was finally finished, Galileo called it *The Assayer*, which referred to the delicate balance used to weigh precious metals. This was a direct response to Grassi's title of *The Astronomical Balance*. *The Assayer* is a manifesto of Galileo's scientific philosophy and method.

The first requirement of a successful scientist, which he referred to as a natural philosopher, is an independence of mind:

> In Sarsi I seem to discern the firm belief that in
> philosophizing one must support oneself upon the
> opinion of some celebrated author, as if our minds
> ought to remain completely sterile and barren unless
> wedded to the reasoning of some other person. Possibly

he thinks that philosophy is a book of fiction . . . in which the least important thing is whether what is written there is true. Well, Sarsi, that is not how matters stand. Philosophy is written in this grand book, the universe, which stands continually open to our gaze. But the book cannot be understood unless one first learns to comprehend the language and reads the letters in which it is composed. It is written in the language of mathematics, and its characters are triangles, circles, and other geometrical figures without which it is humanly impossible to understand a single word of it; without these, one wanders about in a dark labyrinth.

After establishing that a scientist must turn to nature as his teacher and use math as his language, he then makes clear his opinion of those who prefer to follow earlier writers when attacking him:

Perhaps Sarsi believes that all the host of good philosophers may be enclosed within four walls. I believe that they fly, and that they fly alone, like eagles, and not in flocks like starlings. It is true that because eagles are rare birds they are little seen and less heard, while birds that fly like starlings fill the skies with shrieks and cries, and wherever they settle befoul the earth beneath them . . . The crowd of fools who know nothing, Sarsi, is infinite. Those who know very little of philosophy are numerous.

Galileo then pointed out Grassi's misunderstanding of how the telescope worked and the mistakes he made when describing the comet's path. He made it clear, without mentioning Copernicus, that his enemies might be able to temporarily silence him on the unmentioned issue of a moving Earth, but he was still convinced he was right and that, in the end, the truth would win out.

This last point was apparently missed in Rome, where the book was well recieved by many in the Vatican. Cardinal Barberini was particularly impressed and wrote Galileo a glowing letter of praise.

The Assayer was published in May 1623, and Cardinal Barberini wrote his letter to Galileo praising it in late June. Then, in July, Pope Gregory XV, who had succeeded Paul V in 1621, died. In August, Cardinal Barberini was elevated to the papacy. Galileo's old friend was now Pope Urban VIII.

CHAPTER NINE
TWO WORLD SYSTEMS AND A TRIAL

When Cardinal Barberini became Pope Urban VIII the title page of *The Assayer* was changed to include a dedication to the new pope. Urban also appointed several people friendly to Galileo to high positions. The pope's favorite nephew, Francesco Barberini, who had just earned a doctorate at the University of Pisa where he had known the famous Galileo, was made a cardinal. Soon afterward, Galileo received word through Prince Cesi that the pope wanted him to come for a visit.

Ill health and bad weather delayed Galileo's trip to Rome until April 1624. When he arrived, he was warmly received. He had six separate visits with the pope, an impressive gift of the busy pontiff's time.

Pope Urban VIII privately made it clear to Galileo that

he was not going to revisit the 1616 edict against Copernicus. During one of his audiences, Galileo explained his theory of tides and how their motion was evidence of a moving Earth. Urban responded by commenting that God had a multitude of ways to produce the tides and most of these would always be unknown to man.

The pope viewed the 1616 decision as a compromise. Galileo could not prove Copernicus was absolutely true, even with his beloved theory of the tides. Tycho's system also explained the phases of Venus, but without a moving Earth. Because Copernicus could not be proven absolutely, it should only be considered a hypothesis. Galileo also could still not assert that a moving Earth did not conflict with scripture. What did or did not conflict with scripture was a judgement reserved for the Church.

Galileo asked if there was anything wrong in allowing him and others to investigate the question of a moving Earth and to lay the evidence out fairly for all to see. Of course the ultimate authority was God, but was it not the Church's tradition to allow fair-minded men to dispassionately study nature and to arrive at their best conclusions? Before 1616, the Church had not been afraid of what the natural philosophers might discover. Galileo hoped his old friend would restore this tradition by allowing him to write a book comparing the two conflicting theories of Ptolemy and Copernicus. If he could be trusted to write on this subject, it would be a great step toward diminishing the 1616 edict.

Pope Urban agreed that such a book would not violate the 1616 decree—as he understood it—and that it could be a good thing. There was no mention of the unsigned injunction that forbade Galileo to discuss Copernicus in any manner.

At the outset of his years in office, Urban faced more pressing matters than the controversy over Copernicus. The Thirty Years' War had started in 1618 and was still consuming great sections of Central Europe. Urban

When Cardinal Barberini became Pope Urban VIII he granted Galileo permission to write a book comparing the "world systems" of Ptolemy and Copernicus. *(Portrait by Gian Lorenzo Bernini, Courtesy of Galleria Nazionale d'Arte Antica, Rome, Italy.)*

wanted to be the pope who brought the conflict to a victorious end. If he could restore Catholicism as the dominant religion in Europe, he would be the greatest pope since St. Peter. He knew that restoring an atmosphere of intellectual freedom in Italy would make this goal easier. Allowing Galileo to write a book comparing the Ptolemaic and Copernican systems was a way to begin this process.

Galileo had begun a book years before on what he called the two "world systems" of Ptolemy and Copernicus. When he returned home from Rome, he began working on it again. He was facing a daunting challenge. He naturally wanted to make the case for Copernicus, but he had to be careful to not advocate it as an absolute truth. This book would require even more of the subtlety that Galileo employed to such great effect in *The Assayer*.

He wrote the book using the ancient literary device of a dialogue involving three characters. This technique had been used by several philosophers over the centuries. It provided a way for questions to be asked and debated, allowing the author to guide the argument in the direction he chose without ever directly stating his opinion. Galileo's three characters included, Salviati, the committed Copernican who spoke for Galileo and referred to mathematics as the only means of understanding the natural world. His opponent Simplicius, who was just as committed to Aristotle as Salviati was to Copernicus, was modeled on Colombe and the other professors in the Pigeon League. The character in the middle, and the focus of the debate between the other two, was Sagredo, whose name came from a late friend of Galileo's who was remembered as a model of reason and wise judgement.

The book is divided into four days. On day one, the characters discuss Aristotle's physics, with Salviati arguing there is no difference between elements on Earth and in the heavens. The second day's subject is motion and whether Earth spins on its axis. The third day covers astronomy and the question of celestial immutability. Salviati argued Copernicus's system was as logical as, and much simpler than Ptolemy's. The book also revisited the sunspots controversy when Salviati said that it was much easier to understand the motion of the sunspots if Copernicus was correct. On the last day, Galileo turned to his theory of the tides, which Salviati offers as proof that the Earth moves. Interestingly, although Kepler had years earlier established that planets have elliptical orbits , Galileo presents the orbits as circular.

Galileo succeeded in making his *Dialogue* impartial on the surface. No one clearly "wins" the arguments. Simplicius does not hang his head in shame at the end, nor is he made an obvious object of ridicule. Sagredo does not announce at the end that he is convinced of the Copernican system.

Superficially, Galileo stayed within the dictates of the 1616 public decree. He did not do quite as well at abiding by its spirit, however. Over the course of the

The frontispiece of the first edition of Galileo's *Dialogue Concerning the Two Chief World Systems*. *(Courtesy of the University of Toronto, Fisher Rare Book Library.)*

work it becomes clear which position the author supports. Simplicius, for example, consistently justifies his position by referring to ancient texts. Anyone familiar with Galileo knew what he thought of this sort of reasoning. Salviati convincingly countered most of the other Aristotelian concepts that made up the two-sphere universe system.

Dialogue Concerning the Two Chief World Systems was finished in January 1630. The Church had to approve it before it went to press. Galileo arranged for it to be published by the Lincean Academy in Rome, which also meant that a censor in Rome had to approve it. The director of the academy, Prince Cesi, arranged for a Jesuit friend, Father Niccolo Riccardi, to act as censor, ensuring that they would not violate the 1616 edict. Riccardi had performed the same task on *The Assayer*.

In May of 1630, Galileo traveled to Rome to hand over his book to Riccardi. While there, he again met with the pope, who indicated his support for the book's being published once it was approved. Galileo returned to Florence, confident he would soon see his work published and that it would carry the day for Copernicus.

But as they began their work, Riccardi and his assistants grew nervous. They had learned that Galileo's foes were agitated at the prospect of his being allowed to publish a book on astronomy. Father Scheiner and others insisted Galileo had been forbidden from discussing or writing on the topic in any manner. To protect both the author and himself from retribution, Riccardi convinced

Galileo to write a preface that stated clearly the discussion within the book was hypothetical.

In the meantime, Prince Cesi, who provided most of the funding to the Lincean Academy, died suddenly. This left the academy in chaos, and Galileo would have to find a different publisher. He decided to publish in Florence, which meant yet another censor would have to approve the text for licensing in that city, causing further delays. Then the bubonic plague returned, and for months the highways were barricaded and many of the cities quarantined.

The censor in Florence eventually approved the text with only a few changes. In Rome, Riccardi began to doubt the wisdom of going through with the project, and publication was again delayed because of continuing opposition. Galileo would not be deterred, however, and Riccardi was finally convinced to release the manuscript to the printer.

The combination of death, disease, and political wrangling postponed publication until February 1632. Because of the plague, first copies did not arrive in Rome until May of that year. Initial reaction to the work seemed to be very positive, but in only a few weeks' time the storm broke.

In June, Galileo's friend Castelli wrote to recount an anecdote told to him by a bookseller. One afternoon while shopping in Castelli's friend's bookstore, Father Scheiner overheard a priest call *Dialogue* the greatest book ever written. Scheiner reportedly became upset at

The members of the Lincean Academy usually met in this building in Rome.
(Courtesy of Gabinetto delle Stampe, Rome, Italy.)

hearing this and began to shake so violently that the bookseller was alarmed for his health. Scheiner wanted to buy a copy, but it was still in short supply in Rome and there were none available. The agitated Scheiner then offered ten gold ducats, a huge sum, to anyone who would sell him a copy.

By August, Galileo was hearing almost daily reports about efforts to suppress the book. There was also a dangerous, nonscientific subtext to the controversy. The work had been published in Florence, and a serious rift was developing between the pope and the Medici family over the pope's direction of the Vatican's foreign policy concerning the Thirty Years' War. Urban had recently signed a secret agreement with Protestant King Gustavus Adolphus of Sweden and the de facto leader of France, Cardinal Richelieu, to join forces against the Hapsburg rulers of the Holy Roman Empire. The Hapsburgs had, for over a century, been Europe's most loyal supporters of the Counter-Reformation. The war had even spread to Prague, the capital city of Bohemia, with the Protestant majority fighting their Hapsburg rulers.

Although they were joint upholders of Catholicism, a long history of tension existed between the Vatican and the Hapsburgs, who had ruled the Roman Empire for centuries. The Holy Roman Emperor Charles V had even invaded Rome and seized Pope Clement VII in 1527. During the Middle Ages, various Holy Roman emperors had been excommunicated by the pope or threatened with excommunication as a result of the ongoing tension between secular and religious authority.

It was this anxiety about growing Hapsburg power that prompted Urban to make the secret accord with France and Protestant Sweden. Early in the war, the Hapsburgs had been militarily successful against the Protestants in Bohemia and other parts of Germany. Urban was concerned that the conflict would make them too powerful, particularly in northern Italy. It was these geopolitical concerns that led Urban to form an alliance with a Protestant ruler to fight a Catholic empire.

The Medicis were strongly anti-Protestant, so the secret treaty with Sweden angered them, but they reserved their deepest resentment for Cardinal Richelieu of France. Richelieu had recently expelled a member of their family, the former queen Marie de Medici, from France. She had fled to Spain, ruled by a branch of the Hapsburg family, where she was plotting her return to power. Urban, who came from Florence, was well aware of the Medicis' feelings toward Richelieu. The family viewed the treaty as a slap in the face.

The pope's alliance had been made in secret, but it was revealed just as the controversy over *Dialogue Concerning the Two Chief World Systems* was heating up. Because Galileo was an employee of the Medicis, this put him in an unfavorable light. He was also at risk because the Jesuits outnumbered him and were centralized in the Holy City. Scheiner and Grassi, one smarting from the drubbing he took in *Letters on Sunspots*, the other from *The Assayer*, led the anti-Galileans.

Pope Urban was a different man than he had been a few years earlier when, awash in the radiance of having recently become pope, he had offered his hand in friendship to Galileo. By 1632, he was busy with more pressing issues, and he wanted above all to avoid any public fights over Church doctrine. The scandal over Galileo's book could not have come about at a worse time. The Pope was in an uncomfortable position, and it was easier to turn against Galileo than to risk his own reputation by supporting him . In this environment, an appeal to his vanity helped win him over to the anti-Galileo camp.

Grassi and the other Jesuits were able to convince the pontiff that the character Simplicius, who insisted on Ptolemy's system even in the face of overwhelming evidence, was modeled after the pope. They pointed out that it was Simplicius who voiced the Church's official position. Even the argument against Galileo's tide theory, delivered by Simplicius, expressed the Church's position on the theory. Had not this opinion been established by Urban himself? Clearly, Galileo was making a fool of the Holy Pontiff.

There was one final step to sealing Galileo's fate. Urban was shown the addendum to the 1616 edict, which forbade Galileo from so much as discussing Copernicus. Urban reportedly flew into a rage when he read it. He was convinced that Galileo had lied to him during their visit three years before, and that his old friend, knowing he was not supposed to mention the subject, had deliberately kept that information from the pope. Urban could not allow such a transgression to go unpunished.

Urban's reaction was everything Scheiner and Grassi had hoped for. From the pope's perspective, Galileo had tricked him into allowing a work to be published that was in direct conflict with the earlier edict. Then, to add insult to injury, Galileo had tried to make a fool of him in the book. This was a direct challenge to the authority and dignity of the Church.

Galileo became ill when he heard of the pope's reaction. A committee, hastily appointed by Urban and chaired by his nephew Cardinal Francesco Barberini, reported in September that Galileo's book did advocate Copernicus as more than a hypothesis and was therefore in violation of the edict. They recommended that it be suspended but did not suggest any penalties for the author. This decision did not satisfy Urban. He ordered the book suppressed and demanded that the Inquisition bring Galileo to Rome to stand trial for heresy.

Galileo was able to put off leaving home for a few weeks because of his ill health. Then in January he received a warning that he should leave immediately for Rome or he would be taken there forcibly in chains. He embarked on the journey in the dead of winter, sick and unsure if he would ever return to Tuscany. Unable to protect Galileo from the angry pope, the Medicis provided him a litter for transportation to Rome and ordered the Tuscan embassy to make his stay there as comfortable as possible. In Rome, Galileo was nursed and cared for by the Tuscan ambassador and his wife. He was allowed visitors but he did not have freedom to move around the city.

After recovering from his initial shock, Galileo was not overly worried. He expected the book to remain suppressed but believed he could avoid a trial. He had a signed copy of Bellarmino's letter making it clear he could discuss and write about a moving Earth as long as it was treated as a hypothesis. He was certain he had not stepped over this boundary. The suppression was unfortunate, but the book was now in print, and no suppression could get rid of every copy. The book was already being reprinted in Protestant parts of Europe.

On April 12, 1633, Galileo was brought before the officers of the Inquisition, where he was asked a series of questions. Did he remember his 1616 trip to Rome? Did he remember meeting with the cardinals on that visit? Did he remember a discussion about the doctrine of Copernicus? What was his memory of the cardinals' decision regarding Copernicus? To this last question Galileo replied:

> Concerning the controversy that went on about the said opinion of the stability of the Sun and the motion of the Earth it was determined . . . that such an opinion, taken absolutely, is repugnant to Holy Scripture, and it is only to be admitted hypothetically.

This position was the heart of his defense. The 1616 edict had only disallowed the acceptance of Copernicus as an absolute truth, not discussion of it as a theory. To support his position, he gave them a copy of the letter from Bellarmino.

At this point, the Inquisition presented him with a copy of the as yet unmentioned addendum to the original memorandum. Galileo was asked if he remembered this document. Did he see that it specifically forbade him from even discussing the doctrine of Copernicus?

A stunned Galileo could only mumble he had never seen the document before. He had been operating under the dictates of Bellarmino's edict, not this unsigned text, which he claimed to know nothing of before now. This exchange was the core of the trial. Apparently the Inquisition was unaware of the letter from Bellarmino that Galileo had presented, just as he claimed to know nothing of the stricter injunction. The question was whether or not Galileo had knowingly violated the 1616 order. Bellarmino, the only man who could testify as to which

This dramatization of Galileo's trial was painted in the nineteenth century by Robert Fleming. *(Courtesy of Musée du Louvre.)*

letter was real, had died years before. Galileo was never asked to defend the contents of *Dialogue*.

At the conclusion of the interrogation, Galileo was sent back to his quarters. He had received a shock, but all was not lost. The addendum contradicted the public edict as well as the signed letter from Cardinal Bellarmino, but it was unsigned and undated, so Galileo thought it would carry less weight.

The Inquisition was not in the habit of giving up, though. To bring such a prominent man as Galileo all the way to Rome, put him on trial, then announce that there had been a mistake and he was free to go was simply not going to happen. Backing down in that manner would severely weaken the Inquisition's authority. The cardinals began a thorough search for something to support the unsigned addendum. In the meantime, Galileo was kept under house arrest at the embassy.

Over the next days, Galileo began to hear from his friends that the Inquisition was determined to find something on which to convict him and was willing to take as long as necessary to do so. It was possible that new, so-called evidence would surface, which had happened before. The Inquisition had the right to use torture or solitary confinement to wring a confession out of him. They could even begin arresting his friends. Francesco Barberini, who wanted to end this episode as soon as possible, sent word through an intermediary that Galileo should admit to something. Perhaps he could confess to the sins of pride, conceit, and vanity in return for a

This engraving depicts Galileo in his cell, awaiting trial. He actually only spent one night in a cell, and the conditions were not nearly as severe as those represented here. *(Courtesy of the Mansell Collection.)*

lenient sentence. This would let the Inquisition save face, and he could return home. Galileo reluctantly agreed to this arrangement.

Galileo appeared before the Inquisition cardinals again on April 30. He confessed that, after looking over the book, he had erred in advocating Copernicus too strongly and had argued against Ptolemy too severely. He had been vain and overly ambitious. His sin had been a desire to prove he was more clever than others, which had caused him to unwittingly overstep the bounds of the 1616 edict.

On June 21, he was brought back to the Inquisition for a formal interrogation. Under questioning, he claimed to have now rejected Copernicus at the command of the Holy Father. He was there to submit to the will of the Church and to reject all opinions it thought abhorrent to scripture.

That night, Galileo was placed in a cell. The next day, he was brought before the cardinals for sentencing. He had been led to expect a light punishment along with censure of his book. He was instead sentenced to life in prison. Three cardinals, angry at the severity of the sentence, refused to sign the decree.

After rejecting Copernicus again, Galileo was allowed to return to the embassy. On June 26, 1633, Francesco Barberini changed the order of conviction so that Galileo would not have to go to prison. Instead, he would be allowed to serve his sentence under house arrest in Tuscany. The cardinals did not want him to return to the city of Florence too soon, though, fearing he might become a source of agitation. It was arranged through the Tuscan ambassador for Galileo to stay with his friend, Archbishop Piccolomini, at his country estate outside of Siena. Galileo left Rome for the last time and arrived at Piccolomini's estate on July 9, 1633.

CHAPTER TEN
TWO NEW SCIENCES

Galileo was seventy years old when he was sentenced to life imprisonment. His health was bad, and over the remaining nine and half years of his life it would continue to worsen. The long ordeal had also left him emotionally wrecked. Soon after his return to Tuscany, a neighbor of Archbishop Piccolomini wrote, "There were many nights that he did not sleep, but went through the night crying out and rambling so crazily that it was seriously considered whether his arms should be bound."

Galileo remained at Piccolomini's villa four months, gradually recovering his emotional and physical health. The pope heard reports about the large number of visitors he received, but no direct action was taken. Although the Inquisition had won a conviction, they had not been able to remove him from the forefront of science in Italy. There was little to be gained from further aggravating the situation.

In November 1633, Galileo was allowed to return to his own villa, located a few miles from the Convent of San Matteo in Aretri, where his daughter Virginia had taken her vows and assumed the name Maria Celeste. His favorite child, she worried about his illnesses and repaired his clothes. He had made small gifts to the convent over the years and given her money to arrange for a private apartment on the grounds. Now their relationship, carried out by letter, became an important part of his recovery. It did not last long, however, as Maria Celeste died from dysentery in April 1634.

After his daughter's death, Galileo did little work for several weeks. He spent most of his time reading religious literature and sitting in his garden. By the fall of 1634, though, he was ready to resume work.

Galileo did not let his arrest and trial silence him. He was, in a sense, liberated from the controversies and arguments of the past and free to resume the work he had begun as a student in Pisa. At his age, returning to hard work after the trial and while living under house arrest was remarkable; writing a book that is credited by many with founding modern physics is astounding.

The book he wrote in his last years was eventually titled *Discourses and Mathematical Demonstrations Concerning Two New Sciences*. The two new sciences referred to are the static science of the strength of

Galileo's daughter Virginia took the name Maria Celeste when she became a nun. After his trial and sentencing to house arrest, Maria became a great comfort to Galileo. *(Portrait of Maria Celeste by unknown artist. Courtesy of Villa Galletti, Arcetri, Italy.)*

materials and the dynamic science of motion. The book is in some ways a return to the mechanical problems that had occupied him early in his career, including work in the unpublished *On Motion*, written while he was teaching in Pisa. *Two New Sciences* drew on a lifetime of refining his thoughts and techniques on the best way to find scientific truth. Written partly in Italian, *Two New Sciences* also brought back the three characters from *Dialogue* and once again spread their discussion out over four days.

The book begins by discussing the mathematical rules that govern the scaling of objects, which will collapse under their own weight if simply scaled up from smaller models. "Many devices which succeed on a small scale do not work on a large scale," he wrote. It is not enough to simply increase the size, the strength of the material must also be increased proportionately. The three characters then discuss the fulcrum and how weight could be adjusted to avoid fracture. In the process, Galileo lays the groundwork for the development of structural engineering.

The remainder of the work, covering the last three days, deals with motion of various types. On the second day, the characters again discuss falling bodies, which Galileo had studied off and on throughout his entire career. In one passage, Simplicius restates Aristotle's theory that a heavier body falls faster than a lighter body. Salviati's response summarizes Galileo's attitude toward the use of experiments in scientific inquiry:

DISCORSI
E
DIMOSTRAZIONI
MATEMATICHE,
intorno à due nuoue scienze
Attenenti alla
MECANICA & i MOVIMENTI LOCALI,
del Signor
GALILEO GALILEI LINCEO,
Filosofo e Matematico primario del Serenissimo
Grand Duca di Toscana.
Con vna Appendice del centro di grauità d'alcuni Solidi.

IN LEIDA,
Appresso gli Elsevirii. M. D. C. XXXVIII.

The title page of Galileo's last work, *Discourses and Mathematical Demonstrations Concerning Two New Sciences. (Courtesy of University of Toronto, Fisher Rare Book Library.)*

I greatly doubt that Aristotle ever tested by experiment whether it be true that two stones, one weighing ten times as much as the other, if allowed to fall, at the same instant, from a height of, say, 100 cubits, would so differ in speed that when the heavier had reached the ground, the other would not have fallen more than 10 cubits.

Salviati assures Simplicius that "a cannon ball weighing one or two hundred pounds, or even more, will not reach the ground by as much as a span ahead of a musket ball weighing only half a pound, provided both are dropped from a height of 200 cubits." Aristotle had never tested his theory of falling bodies. If he had, he would likely have revised it based on his observations. In other words, if Aristotle were alive, even he would not be an Aristotelian as the Peripatetics defined it.

When he turned to projectiles, Galileo revamped another aspect of Aristotle's physics. As noted earlier, Aristotle had divided motion into two types—natural motion and violent motion—and said that no object could experience different motions at the same time. This meant that the motion of any projectile, such as a released arrow or a thrown ball, was divided into two parts. The first motion, which resulted from the initial impetus—the releasing of the bowstring, for example— was a violent motion that continued until the initial impetus was exhausted. At that point, natural motion took over and the projectile fell to the ground. However, anyone who has shot an arrow or thrown a ball can see that the projectile does not suddenly drop, but falls in a downward arc. Another question that had perplexed Aristotelians for centuries was where exactly did the violent motion end and the natural motion take over?

Using the acceleration ratio of distance to time developed in his work on falling bodies, Galileo explained the relationship between the projectile's forward motion, triggered by the initial impetus, and the rate of fall that occurred after the initial impetus ended. He used a mathematical model to describe how projectiles travel in a single parabolic path, not in two distinct phases. Motion, he said, was a factor of impetus, weight, and resistance. An arrow leaves the bow, arcs higher at a rate dependent on the force of the impetus, and continues the arc as it falls to the ground at an accelerating speed.

In this discussion of projectiles, Galileo came close to developing a new law of inertia. Aristotle had said all bodies were naturally at rest, and motion was the result of impetus. Once a body was set in motion it sought to return to rest. To the contrary, Galileo wrote that a projectile continued in motion until another force stopped it; there was no inherent tendency within the object to return to rest. Just as a projectile remained motionless until impetus was applied, it would remain airborne until another force returned it to rest. Inertia was not only a state of rest, but of motion as well. Galileo limited his discussion of inertia to projectiles on Earth. Later, Isaac Newton would pick up on this revision of the law of inertia and apply it to the entire universe.

Two New Sciences explains how Galileo thought mathematics should be used to understand and describe physical phenomena. Experiments are best used to test a mathematically conceived hypothesis. It was also possible to begin from a theoretical perspective and then develop a thought experiment that could be subjected to mathematical analysis. An actual experiment was valuable, in this controlled manner, as a way of validating the mathematical hypothesis. Valuable scientific research was a combination of intuition, observation, mathematical analysis, and experimentation.

As he worked on *Two New Sciences*, a parade of visitors, including former students and supporters, visited Galileo at his villa. The Inquisition was aware that he was working again, but made no overt attempts to stop

British scientist Isaac Newton incorporated Galileo's work on motion and force into his famous Three Laws of Motion. *(Portrait by Kneller, 1702. Courtesy of National Portrait Gallery, London, U.K.)*

him. The trial and conviction of its greatest scientist had stalled scientific research in Italy. As prominent individuals saw the Protestant areas of Europe, particularly England, moving ahead scientifically, sympathy grew for what many saw as the unjust treatment of Galileo.

When *Two New Sciences* was completed, Galileo faced the problem of where to have it published. Because he was not allowed to publish in Italy, his friends began to look abroad for a patron willing to finance printing. Eventually, Louis Elzevir, a Dutch Protestant printer, agreed to take on the project. The manuscript was smuggled to Holland, where it was published in 1638.

Around this time, the English poet John Milton visited Galileo. Later, he wrote about Galileo as an example of how Italian scholars suffered during the Inquisition.

Even before he finished work on *Two New Sciences,* Galileo began his final descent into blindness. He had been troubled by his eyes for some time, and this new onset apparently began with an infection. In 1637, he was allowed to move to Florence to live with his son. His

eyes continued to fail until he lost sight in first the left eye, then the right. By December 1637, he was totally blind.

In June 1639, Galileo returned to his country villa. Because he was in need of constant care, his son and some former students joined him there. He tried to re-sume work by dictating notes based on his motion research.

Poet John Milton visited Galileo near the end of the scientist's life. *(Artist unknown.)*

Galileo continued to work through declining health and blindness until, in 1641, he was forced to bed with heart and kidney trouble. He was in constant pain and was usually feverish. He could eat little and, denied his beloved wine by the doctors, subsisted mostly on water.

Galileo Galilei died on the evening of January 8, 1642. He was seventy-nine. Pope Urban refused to allow a funeral oration or the construction of a monument honoring his old friend. Galileo was buried in a crypt at the Church of Santa Croce in Florence.

Opposite: This portrait of Galileo was painted in 1636, by Justus Sustermans. *(Courtesy of Galleria degli Uffizi, Florence, Italy.)*

Galileo Galilei is one of only a handful of historical figures who are referred to by first name—an indication of the important role he played in the development of modern science. His work in physical mechanics and his insistence on using experiment along with the quantification of results make him a truly pivotal figure.

Galileo's influence extends beyond the scientific method, though. The story of his conflict with religious authority and the intellectual institutions of Italy has become one of the archetypal stories of the modern world, although it is often misunderstood in its detail. He was arrested, tried, and convicted for advocating a scientific idea deemed contrary to the Christian religion. This situation established the notion in the minds of many that there is an unavoidable conflict between science and religion. What is often lost in the story, though, is that Galileo argued that the conflict between the two was neither inherent nor unavoidable. The problem was in the failure of man's mind and imagination, he asserted, not God's.

Galileo could probably have avoided open conflict with the Church, as many scientists before and after him managed to do. Instead, he chose to maintain a high-profile public position, ultimately at his own peril. While it can be argued that he brought a great deal of his trouble onto himself, it is also true that his example effectively announced to the world that a new era had begun. Science had moved into a central place in human life and in human consciousness—a position it continues to occupy in the twenty-first century.

TIMELINE

1564 Galileo Galilei is born on February 15 in Pisa, Italy.

1574 Joins his family in Florence, Italy.

1581 Attends University of Pisa to study medicine.

1582 Ostilio Ricci introduces Galileo to mathematics.

1585 Leaves University of Pisa without a medical degree.

1588 Returns to University of Pisa as chairman of mathematics.

1592 Becomes chair of mathematics at the University of Padua.

1609 Uses telescope to observe the moon, and the moons of Jupiter.

1610 Appointed mathematician to the Medici family and professor of philosophy and mathematics at the University of Pisa; returns to Florence.

1611 First visit to Rome; becomes member of the Academy of the Lincei.

1615 Returns to Rome.

1616 The Inquisition places Nicholas Copernicus's *On Revolutions of the Heavenly Spheres* on suspended list, and Galileo is forbidden to write or teach Copernicus's ideas as absolute truth or compatible with scripture.

1624 Pope Urban VIII requests a visit by Galileo in Rome.

1632 Pope Urban VIII demands Galileo return to Rome; Galileo tried by the Inquisition.

1633 The Inquisition sentences Galileo to life in prison, which was commuted to house arrest.

1642 Galileo dies on January 8, at the age of seventy-nine.

SOURCES

CHAPTER TWO: "On Motion"

p. 28, "Try, if you can, to picture . . ." Galileo Galilei, *Dialogue concerning the two chief world systems, Ptolemaic & Copernican*, trans. Stillman Drake, (Berkeley: University of California Press, 1953), 223.

p. 28, "Aristotle says that a hundred-pound ball . . ." Galileo Galilei, *Two new sciences, including centers of gravity & force of percussion*, trans. Stillman Drake (Madison: University of Wisconsin Press, 1974), 68.

CHAPTER THREE: "Starry Messenger"

p. 43, "marvelous and effective singularity . . ." S.A. Bedini, *Galileo, Man of Science*, ed. E. McMullin (New York: Basic Books, 1967), 269.

p. 46, "I have preferred not to publish . . ." Stillman Drake, *Galileo at Work: his scientific biography* (Chicago: University of Chicago Press, 1978), 41.

p. 48, "rough and uneven . . ." Galileo Galilei, "The Starry Messenger," in *Discoveries and Opinions of Galileo*, trans. Stillman Drake (New York: Doubleday, 1957), 28.

p. 50, "Why should I not believe . . ." Dava Sobel, *Galileo's Daughter* (New York: Walker Publishing, 1999), 35.

CHAPTER FOUR: "Phases of Venus"

p. 52, "I have experienced . . ." Sobel, *Galileo's Daughter*, 38.

CHAPTER FIVE: "Bodies in Water"

p. 64, "The hypothesis is pretty; its only fault . . ." Drake, *Galileo at Work*, 169.

CHAPTER SIX: "Sunspots"

p. 73, "I . . . must be more cautious . . ." Galileo Galilei, "Letters on Sunspots," in *Discoveries and Opinions of Galileo*, trans. Stillman Drake (New York: Doubleday, 1957), 90.

p. 75, "With absolute necessity . . ." Ibid., 94.

p. 77, A certain crowd . . . Sobel, *Galileo's Daughter*, 45.

CHAPTER SEVEN: "Defeat in Rome"

p. 91, "the Earth moves around the Sun . . ." Drake, *Galileo at Work*, 348.

CHAPTER EIGHT: "Assayer"

p. 92, "In the palace and residence . . ." Drake, *Galileo at Work*, 348.

p. 95, "Now, since I know . . ." Ludovico Geymonat. *Galileo Galilei: A Biography and Inquiry into His Philosophy of Science*, trans. Stillman Drake (New York: McGraw-Hill, 1965), 95.

p. 97, "As a result . . ." Sobel, *Galileo's Daughter*, 85.

p. 102, "anomalous illuminations in the air." Ibid., 89.

p. 103, "But suppose we grant . . ." *The Controversy on the comets of 1618; Galileo Galilei, Horatio Grassi, Mario Guiducci, Johann Kepler*, trans. Stillman Drake and C.D. O'Malley (Philadelphia: University of Pennsylvania Press, 1960), 71.

p. 103, "In Sarsi I seem to discern . . ." Ibid., 183.

CHAPTER NINE: "Two World Systems and a Trial"

p. 119, Concerning the controversy . . . Drake, *Galileo at Work*, 345.

CHAPTER TEN: "Two New Sciences"

p. 124, "There were many nights . . ." Drake, *Galileo at Work*, 353.

p. 127, "Many devices which succeed on a small scale do not work on a large scale," he wrote. Galileo, *Two new sciences*, 93.

p. 128, "I greatly doubt . . ." *Dialogue Concerning Two New Sciences*, trans. Henry Crew and Alfonso de Salvio (New York: The Macmillan Company, 1914), 61.

BIBLIOGRAPHY

Bedini, S.A. *Galileo, Man of Science*. Ed. E. McMullin. New York: Basic Books, 1967.

De Santillana, Giorgio. The Crime of Galileo. Chicago: University of Chicago Press, 1955.

Drake, Stillman. *Galileo at Work: his scientific biography*. Chicago: University of Chicago Press, 1978.

———. *Galileo: Pioneer Scientist*. Toronto: University of Toronto Press, 1990.

Galilei, Galileo. *The Controversy on the comets of 1618; Galileo Galilei, Horatio Grassi, Mario Guiducci, Johann Kepler*. Trans. Stillman Drake and C.D. O'Malley. Philadelphia: University of Pennsylvania Press, 1960.

———. *Dialogue concerning the two chief world systems, Ptolemaic & Copernican*. Trans. Stillman Drake, ed. Giorgio de Santillana. Berkeley: University of California Press, 1953.

———. *Dialogue Concerning Two New Sciences*. Trans. Henry Crew and Alfonso de Salvio. New York: The Macmillan Company, 1914.

———. *Discoveries and Opinions of Galileo*. Trans. Stillman Drake. New York: Doubleday, 1957.

———. *Two new sciences, including centers of gravity & force of percussion*. Trans. Stillman Drake. Madison: University of Wisconsin Press, 1974.

Geymonat, Ludovico. *Galileo Galilei: A Biography and Inquiry into His Philosophy of Science*. Trans. Stillman Drake. New York: McGraw-Hill, 1965.

Redondi, Pietro. *Galileo: Heretic*. Trans. Raymond Rosenthal. Princeton: Princeton University Press, 1989.

Sharrat, Michael. *Galileo—Decisive Innovator*. Oxford: Blackwell, 1994.

Sobel, Dava. *Galileo's Daughter*. New York: Walker Publishing, 1999.

WEBSITES

The Galileo Project, Rice University
http://es.rice.edu/ES/humsoc/Galileo/

The Institute and Museum of the History of Science, Florence, Italy
http://galileo.imss.firenze.it/

Museum of the History of Science, Oxford, United Kingdom
http://www.mhs.ox.ac.uk/

INDEX